PENGUIN PASSNOTES

The Pardoner's Tale

Dr Graham Handley has taught and lectured for over thirty years. He was Principal Lecturer in English and Head of Department at the College of All Saints, Tottenham, and Research Officer in English, Birkbeck College, University of London. He is a part-time Lecturer in Literature with the University of London Department of Extramural Studies and also teaches part-time at Enfield Chace Upper School. He has examined at all levels from CSE to University Honours Degree, and has published on Dickens, Mrs Gaskell and George Eliot. He has edited *The Mill on the Floss* and *Wuthering Heights* for Macmillan and *Daniel Deronda* for the Clarendon Press, Oxford. He has written studies of *The Go-Between* and *To Kill a Mockingbird* for the Pass-notes series and of *Vanity Fair* for the Masterstudies series.

PENGUIN PASSNOTES

GEOFFREY CHAUCER

The Pardoner's Tale

GRAHAM HANDLEY

ADVISORY EDITOR: STEPHEN COOTE, M.A., PH.D.

PENGUIN BOOKS

PENGUIN BOOKS

Published by the Penguin Group
27 Wrights Lane, London W8 5TZ, England
Viking Penguin Inc., 40 West 23rd Street, New York, New York 10010, USA
Penguin Books Australia Ltd, Ringwood, Victoria, Australia
Penguin Books Canada Ltd, 2801 John Street, Markham, Ontario, Canada L3R 1B4
Penguin Books (NZ) Ltd, 182–190 Wairau Road, Auckland 10, New Zealand

Penguin Books Ltd, Registered Offices: Harmondsworth, Middlesex, England

First published 1986
Reprinted 1988

Made and printed in Great Britain by
Richard Clay Ltd, Bungay, Suffolk
Filmset in Monophoto Ehrhardt

The copy text used for this edition is that of the second edition of
The Complete Works of Geoffrey Chaucer, *edited by Rev. W. W Skeat,*
published by Oxford at the Clarendon Press.

For Jeff Ace, with affectionate gratitude

Contents

Introduction

CHAUCER'S LIFE AND WORKS

Geoffrey Chaucer was born about 1340, the son of John Chaucer, a prosperous London wine-merchant. The known facts of his life – for example, details of his education – are sparse, but scholars have been able to deduce much about him. He obviously read widely from an early age, mastering Latin as well as French and English. He became familiar with Ovid, Virgil and many other Latin writers, was a student of French literature, and his knowledge of Italian is shown in his acquaintance with the works of Dante and Boccaccio.

The earliest records of Chaucer are to be found in the financial accounts of the Duke of Clarence's wife in 1357. These show that money was spent on clothing for him, an indication that he was in her service, though his position is not defined. While in the Duchess's service he probably met his future wife. He went to France in 1359 with the army of Edward III and, while the King was laying siege to Rheims, Chaucer was taken prisoner. He was ransomed in the following year, the King paying some £16 towards his freedom. Soon afterwards he was employed as a messenger bearing letters from those negotiating with the French at Calais to England, and for the next few years he may well have been in the King's employment. By 1366 he was married. His wife Philippa was in the service of the Queen, from whom in 1366 she received an annuity in her married name.

In June 1367 Chaucer became a yeoman of the King, and in the following year he appears among the esquires. The latter were personal attendants upon the King, but they were also employed on diplomatic missions abroad. Chaucer was obviously considered responsible enough for such tasks, and was abroad in 1366, 1368 and 1370 on unspecified duty. In the 1370s he was sent to Flanders,

France and Italy. His visits to the latter country certainly influenced his literary career. The first was probably in December 1372. It lasted until the middle of the following year, and its main purpose was to provide an English port as a base for Genoese merchants. He also visited Florence. In 1378 he journeyed to Italy again, almost certainly with the object of obtaining military help in the war against France.

In 1374 Chaucer leased a house over Aldgate in London, and in June of that year he was appointed Controller of Customs. Eight years later he acquired a similar post. In 1385 he was allowed to perform his duties through the delegation of work to a deputy, and he held both these Customs offices until the end of 1386. These twelve years were prosperous for Chaucer, and in 1386 he was appointed a Justice of the Peace for Kent, where he had taken up residence. He was also elected as a Member of Parliament in that year, though his period of service was a brief one.

His wife died in 1387, and Chaucer appears to have gone through a period of financial embarrassment and political decline. He sold his annuities in 1388, and in the same year some of his friends suffered execution for treason as the Duke of Gloucester sought to establish his ascendancy over the King. It was not until May 1389 that the King (Richard II) reasserted his royal prerogative. Chaucer benefited almost immediately, being appointed Clerk of the Works at Westminster and being given responsibility for the royal manors and lodges. In 1390 he undertook comprehensive surveying duties for the King, suffered a double robbery, and gave up his clerkship in 1391. He continued to work for the King, receiving a gift from Richard in 1393 'for his good service in the present year'. In 1394 he was granted a new annuity of £20 and in 1398 an annual gift of wine.

There is some evidence that he may have needed ready money from time to time, since a number of advances on his annuity are recorded, and he was at least once sued for debt.

Although Richard II was deposed by Henry of Lancaster in 1399 (Henry IV), the new king confirmed the grants made to Chaucer by Richard and added one of his own. At Christmas 1399 Chaucer leased a house in the garden of St Mary's chapel, Westminster Abbey, but he only lived until 25 October 1400. He was buried in Westminster Abbey.

That Chaucer's was a busy life until his latter years there can be no doubt. His poetry was written for courtly audiences and established his success as a story-teller. What he also achieved through his poetry was the assimilation of the literature of other languages – Latin, French, Italian – into English. It is important to remember that medieval poetry was oral, and Chaucer as a squire was required to read poetry – sometimes his own – to his royal patrons, as a contemporary manuscript illustration of him standing at a lectern shows. Remember always that Chaucer's poetry was for the ear rather than the eye, for manuscripts were expensive to produce. Chaucer's early poems show evidence of the French literary tradition and more particularly the influence of the thirteenth-century French poem the *Roman de la Rose*. In his own *The Legend of Good Women* he refers to a translation of this, but only a fragment of the surviving translation is thought to be by Chaucer.

Chaucer's first major poem was *The Book of the Duchess* which was written in 1370 about the death of Blanche, Duchess of Lancaster, the wife of Chaucer's patron, John of Gaunt. It is an allegory, which is the description of a subject under the guise of another subject, here one of aptly suggestive resemblance. The narrator is a mask for Chaucer himself. It is important as it is the first time he uses a device which he was to employ again, nowhere better than in the Canterbury pilgrim who tells the story behind the stories of *The Canterbury Tales*. Typically, and even this early, the poem has some of those comic and ironic qualities which again characterize *The Canterbury Tales*.

Chaucer's next poem, *The House of Fame*, was not finished, but the literary and narrative elements are both serious and comic, the latter being particularly present in colloquial sequences. Also in the dream-allegorical mode is *The Parliament of Fowls*. Both *The House of Fame* and *The Book of the Duchess* were written in rhyming couplets like those used in *The Pardoner's Tale*, but *The Parliament of Fowls* is in seven-line verses.

The Legend of Good Women is also cast in the dream form in the prologue. Here couplets are again used, the prologue containing a beautiful sequence in worship of the daisy at the beginning of May. The stories told by Chaucer are of heroines who suffered for or who died on their lovers' accounts. In brief it is an adaptation, the lives of these pagan ladies replacing the Christian lives of saints which were a commonplace of the times. Almost inevitably the treatment is somewhat monotonous, and Chaucer obviously lost interest in relating the lesser-known legends. The material is drawn largely from Virgil and Ovid and the poem, like *The House of Fame*, is unfinished.

The narrative poem *Troilus and Criseyde* is a masterpiece by any standards, combining high (and dramatic) narrative art, a skilful and sustained use of stanza form, a superb control of dialogue and, perhaps above all, psychological penetration in the depiction of character. It appears to be a mature work, perhaps written sometime in the 1380s. It is a courtly-love poem, that is, a poem which embodies an idealized view of love, with the knight worshipping his lady at a distance, praying for her, weeping for her, pledging his eternal faithfulness. The pagan story has the medieval framework and, ultimately, like *The Legend of Good Women*, what F. N. Robinson rightly calls 'Chaucer's essentially religious spirit'. Running through the poem is a strong assertion of the power of fate, and Troilus actually speaks of predestination. The ending shows the author asserting the power and the duty of religious love as against earthly love.

The Canterbury Tales

Chaucer's greatest work appears to have largely been written in his later years, though some sections of it certainly belong to an early period. The *General Prologue* to the *Tales* was written in 1387. This *Prologue*, which runs to 860 lines, is much more than a preface to the Tales. It is a detailed description of the pilgrims as they make their way to the holy shrine at Canterbury. (See separate section on *The Canterbury Pilgrimage*.)

Some of the *Tales* have been dated as late as 1393–94. The collection is unfinished, and there is an indication, as with some of the other poems, that Chaucer's interest in the scheme waxed and waned. Perhaps it was that the mammoth nature of the task – upward of 150 tales were projected – could never be translated into practical reality. For an account of *The Prologue to the Canterbury Tales* students should consult Stephen Coote's study of it in the Penguin *Passnotes* edition which has both commentary and text.

The idea of a general framework which encloses the telling of stories had precedents in classical and contemporary literature and in Chaucer's own *The Legend of Good Women*. Chaucer was able to bring together a cross-section of the society of the time, and to show them in interaction with one another on the way to the shrine. Each of the tales reflects something of the character telling it, and each in fact reflects Chaucer's infinite variety – his ability to be colloquial, elevated, humorous, even coarse, moral and philosophical. Above all it shows him as a sophisticated teller of tales, adapting and creating with narrative verve.

There seems to be evidence that Chaucer drew some of his portraits from life, hence the animation and vividness of his characters. Harry Bailly, the Host, probably derives from an innkeeper at Southwark, the Shipman from Peter Risshenden, while the Man of Law was probably the real life Sergeant-at-Law, Thomas Pinchbeck. The reality of the pilgrims lies in their common humanity, whether it is frail, loud, coarse or noble. To take some examples, it is fitting that the Knight should be described first, since he is the most eminent in terms of career, status and moral precepts – he is chivalrous, modest, courageous, a man of honour who is well-bred, well-behaved and generous. He is the model Christian, treating all alike regardless of what we would call class. His is a natural humility which rejects ostentation in dress or behaviour. The Squire is a young nobleman, a fashionable dresser, accomplished enough to write lyrics and to play an instrument. He is so much in love that he can't sleep at night, but he displays qualities of modesty and obedience which show that he is truly the Knight's son. The class range is extended by the Yeoman, servant to the Knight, a forester, a skilled craftsman devoted to that craft and to his religion. It will be apparent from the above that Chaucer has taken three types, imbued them with a strong and re-cognizable individuality yet at the same time made them representative of certain moral and practical qualities.

Of the 'religious' pilgrims, the Pardoner is placed last in Chaucer's list, a placing which will be examined on page 15. The Prioress has claims to be a lady, her table manners exemplifying her sense of refinement and over-exaggerated delicacy. She has a kind of harmless snobbery. The Monk, on the other hand, represents the worldliness of the Church. He has a good appetite, is full of life and energy and devotes himself to hunting, his favourite occupation. He is the reverse of those who sincerely follow their religious vocation, since poverty, chastity and obedience, the triple vow of the true monk, have no part in his observance. The Friar too is intent on worldliness, advancing himself by courting the rich and offering absolution for payment. He is a hypocrite who lives for pleasure, tricking the poor and ingratiating himself with the women by providing gifts. Yet such is Chaucer's tone that the portrait of the Friar is not condemnatory; he is vibrant, colourful and a likeable rogue.

The Clerk is unworldly, interested in study to the exclusion of material possessions or of advancement in the Church. He prays for others, speaks but briefly and learnedly, and is himself prepared to pass on what he has learned as well as learning from others.

The poor Parson is learned and full of holy thoughts and actions, devout, dedicated, kind, a truly practising Christian who shared with his poor and visited all regardless of distance. He set a Christian example for all to follow. The description is sympathetic and warm. Chaucer enlarges on the essential goodness of this priest, who has the sincerity and integrity to reprove the sinful and maintain his Christian standards and function regardless of circumstances. The author's own sincerity, his own Christian faith and stance, is shown in such lines as

> A bettre preest, I trowe that nowher noon is.

The concluding couplet puts the seal on the portrait:

> But Cristes lore, and his apostles twelve,
> He taughte, and first he folwed it him-selve.

The Summoner – a person responsible for bringing people charged with offences before an ecclesiastical court – rides with the Pardoner. He is so unattractive that children are frightened by his appearance. He is hot-blooded from eating garlic and leeks, lecherous and loves coarse red wine which produces a violent reaction in him. He pretends to learning by quoting Latin phrases, but is an ignorant man in reality. He is a rogue, and can be bribed with wine to excuse the sins of the flesh, but he knows all about the people in his area.

The account of the Pardoner is given elsewhere in this commentary, and we should perhaps stress here again that it is significant that he is the last to be described apart from the host, Harry Bailly, almost as if he is the least worthy, because of his profession, to be on this pilgrimage. The author says that he intends to describe the journey and the rest of the pilgrimage, and apologizes in advance for any emphases his story may take. The host, who is a cheerful and intelligent man, provides the idea of the pilgrims each telling stories to the others to pass away the time on the journey to Canterbury and back. The one to 'telleth in this cas/Tales of best sentence and most solas' will have a supper bought by all the others as a reward. The host then offers to go with the pilgrims and be their guide, and the following morning they set off, having first drawn lots to see who is to tell the first Tale. The Knight draws the shortest straw and begins his tale 'with right a mery chere'. It is not my intention in this brief account to summarize each of the tales, but rather to indicate in passing the variety and quality of a selection of them in order to emphasize the nature of Chaucer's achievement both as a narrative artist and in terms of the picture he gives of his times, his own moral or religious viewpoint, if you like, the position of the teller of all the tales, the author himself. Chaucer is capable of coarse and colloquial humour and high tragedy, of painting a picture or drawing a cartoon, of directness and subtlety, and the tales exemplify all the characteristics mentioned above and more.

The Knight's Tale: It is fitting both in terms of status and character that the Knight should tell the first story. His is a Tale of chivalry and romance in which Palamon and Arcite compete for the love of Emily, the sister of Hyppolita, the Queen of the Amazons who has married Theseus. Though comments in the Chaucerian voice provide a contemporary reference from time to time, the story itself is remote from contemporary experience. The Tale is a fine example of the courtly literature of the time. So many-sided and various is Chaucer that it appears likely he took the tale and gave it his own individuality, pointing up the beauty, humour *and* the conflict and suffering at the same time.

The Miller's Tale: The drunken Miller insists on telling a 'noble tale' to cap that of the Knight. It is in fact coarse, humorous, sexual and scurrilous, the very antithesis of *The Knight's Tale*, immediate evidence of Chaucer's relaxed capacity to work by contrast. Chaucer is able to use, here in comic vein, the influence of astrology on the

minds of people in his time. What is important is the vivid characterization, the speed and coarseness of the comedy, the reader being
involved in a constant sense of anticipation at what will happen next.
The belly chuckle is complemented by the sheer verve of the story
and, unlike the previous tale, there is a sense of realism, of actuality,
throughout.

The *Prologue* to *The Wife of Bath's Tale*, like *The Miller's Tale*,
gives the impression of being rooted in actuality, the vivacious account
of the Wife's five husbands and her reduction of them supporting
her twin assertions that marriage should not be held inferior to vir-
ginity, and that sovereignty in the marriage relationship should belong
to the wife.

The Tale which follows her superb Prologue serves as a demonstration of the Wife's argument. Chaucer's technique here invites
comparison with *The Pardoner's Tale*, since the Pardoner's sermon
on a given text ironically demonstrates his own surrender to the
principles he is condemning in others. The vivacity of the Prologue is
followed by the skilful narrative of the Tale. This is structurally neat,
with a combination of life experience supported by fictional illustration.

The Nun's Priest's Tale, like *The Pardoner's Tale*, further instances
Chaucer's range and variety and it is also a sermon. Adapted from
various stories of the Fox and the Cock, it displays a brilliant origi-
nality in the use of the material. The focus is on a poor widow's cock
Chanticleer and his beautiful hen Pertelot at a time when, the priest
tells his audience, birds and animals could sing. Chanticleer confides
to Pertelot a dream he has had of an animal which seized him. Later
he sees a fox lying in the vegetables, and is unwisely flattered into
opening his mouth to sing. He closes his eyes to sing the better, and is
seized by the fox. But he keeps his presence of mind, persuades the
fox to open his mouth to announce that he is going to eat him
forthwith, and escapes when the fox does so. The priest takes the
moral of the Tale from St Paul – what was set down in the past (here
the powerful accuracy of dreams) was written for our benefit, and we
should not ignore it.

These four Tales provide interesting points of contrast with *The
Pardoner's Tale*, and at the same time they indicate Chaucer's variety
in terms of verse usage, treatment and themes. *The Knight's Tale*

employs the courtly-love theme we have noted earlier, with idealized figures but the same mastery of the rhyming couplet which is present in *The Pardoner's Tale*. The emphasis is on nobility and the influence of fate. *The Pardoner's Tale*, by way of contrast, is thoroughly ignoble in terms of the character who tells the story and the characters and their actions in the story, while the theme that money is the root of all evil is the very opposite of the idea of fate, since the man who chooses to be greedy (or who indulges any of the other sins) is making his own fate in the eyes of God.

The Miller's Tale contains a degree of coarseness matched only by the remarks of the Host at the end of *The Pardoner's Tale*. The other points of contrast are not marked. If the sin is adultery, then it is punished, but the tone is humorous throughout. *The Wife of Bath's Tale* contains many learned references to underline the main theme that in marriage the sovereignty should be with the wife. *The Nun's Priest's Tale* has many correspondences with *The Pardoner's Tale*, for it is a sermon on, for example, the sins of lust and pride. The Nun's Priest himself asserts that the 'moralitee' of his Tale contains a warning against carelessness, the neglect of one's duty and the lures of flattery. The Tale ends with three lines of blessing or prayer as in a sermon, and these lines are comparable to the Pardoner's three lines of blessing in his own sermon (see text lines 588–90):

> Now, gode god, if that it be thy wille,
> As seith my lord, so make us alle good men:
> And bringe us to his heighe blisse. Amen.

Chaucer is both various and particular, and *The Pardoner's Tale* has the sharp focus and the narrative flair which characterize the Tales mentioned above.

CHAUCER'S TIMES

It is not my concern here to examine the political background to Chaucer's maturity except by glancing at major events where they shed light on some relevant aspect of medieval life. Some knowledge of that life is important to our understanding of Chaucer, for great writers are of their time and must necessarily reflect it in some ways. Leaving aside the Court, the class structure is reflected in the three estates represented in *The Canterbury Tales*, with the Knight standing for the first or noble estate, the various characters of the Church the second estate, and the third comprising the working men (not working-class in our modern sense) from, for example, the Merchant to the Ploughman.

The England of the period was a largely agricultural country, in the approximate ratio of nine-tenths villagers to one-tenth town-dwellers. These villages, generally having a population of about two hundred, were often self-sufficient, their occupants rarely if ever going even as far as a market town. In some instances their only visitors during the year would be pedlars. From the priest to a number of manual trades involving farming or carpentry, they lived for the most part in thatched houses, which could be moved if necessary to a new location.

In *The Prologue to the Canterbury Tales* both the portrait of the Reeve (a manager of a large estate) and the Franklin (a man owning a large area of land but not himself of noble birth) testify to Chaucer's awareness of the contemporary social scene away from the Court he knew so well. His range is various and the poor Parson and the Ploughman, for example, are what have been appropriately called the 'twin pillars of the village at its best'.

In *The Pardoner's Tale* there is a passing but significant reference to the Plague, and although the formal setting of his Tale is Flanders, I think we can accept this as a contemporary reference. Bubonic plague – known as the Black Death – had appeared in England in 1348, when Chaucer was a child. Up to fifty per cent of the population, varying according to locality but sometimes ninety per cent in one area, were killed. The Pardoner mentions diseases in cattle and sheep, which would be common at the time. In fact, the conception of a population many of whom lived at a very low level of subsistence and were prone to illness is from time to time apparent in *The Canterbury Tales*, and here Chaucer is certainly holding up the mirror to his own times in the country area.

Of the large towns, London was then as now the centre, not merely of the Court but of trade. The aldermen of the food trade had legislative powers, and the cloth guilds, particularly towards the end of the fourteenth century, also increased in stature and influence. With the expansion of sheep-farming the wool trade increased too, particularly in the west of England, with Bristol as the greatest port for the export trade. The value of wool is shown in *The Wife of Bath's Tale*, for the Wife is a great trader. There is also a mention in *The Pardoner's Tale*, where the Pardoner urges wives to make offerings of wool and also indicates his liking for it.

There is little mention in Chaucer's poetry of the political events of the time, and when we remember that this was the period which saw the struggle for power between Richard II and the Duke of Gloucester, we feel that Chaucer was perhaps too close to the events of the day to comment on them. The Pardoner and his practices were specifically of Chaucer's time, both before it and after it, the office of Pardoner continuing to exist until its final abolition at the Council of Trent in 1562. The next section of this commentary will consider the importance of the Church in Chaucer's time (with particular reference to the 'religious' characters in *The Prologue to the Canterbury Tales*) and the relationship of the Pardoners to that Church. In that tale Chaucer is exposing an abuse in the individual, his office and in the Church itself.

THE CANTERBURY PILGRIMAGE

The pilgrimage reflects the religious climate of the time, where all activity is dominated by the influence of the Catholic Church. The pilgrims, whether idealized or real or seen ironically, represent a cross-section of medieval life, and the idea of a pilgrimage provides Chaucer with the basic framework for the telling of a series of tales. Harry Bailly, the Host, is the constant presence, acting as organizer and umpire at one and the same time, but the important thing to remember is that the ordinary medieval mind related all life experiences to religious interpretation. Events in life were thus seen as being a manifestation of biblical or supernatural truth.

The pilgrimage was a common expression of religious feeling focused on a particular shrine in medieval England, with that of St Thomas à Becket providing a natural expression of man's devotion to

God and of his search for spiritual solace. Becket was the Archbishop of Canterbury who was murdered in 1170. Quite simply, he had dared to threaten the authority of that King (Henry II) with the greater authority of the Church. He was regarded by some as a traitor, by others as a martyr, but two centuries after his death there had built up around him a collection of stories regarding his relics. These were said to work miracles, to achieve cures, to raise up the dead. His shrine was the most popular in England, pilgrims assembling and descending on Canterbury, in Chaucer's words, 'The holy blisful martir for to seke' out of gratitude for what they believed the saint had done. But any pilgrimage would contain individuals with a mixture of motives, from the devout and the sincere to the opportunist out for a good time. Chaucer's gathering contains saints and sinners and many in-betweens, and in this way he is reflecting a truth about people and about life. However serious the purpose of a pilgrimage, it consisted of people who were going for pleasure and indeed often for company, as witness the Wife of Bath, as well as those whose motives were exclusively spiritual. That the Pardoner should be on the pilgrimage reflects Chaucer's ironic presentation of character and motive. The Pardoner is stocked with fake relics calculated to delude the gullible; the pilgrims are intent on what is for them – and perhaps for Chaucer – the real and efficacious relics of a real saint. The overall serious purpose of the pilgrimage is exemplifed in such idealized characters as the poor Parson and the Knight; the Pardoner is the salesman who is travelling for earthly profit, though (and this shows another layer of the Chaucerian irony) his cautionary Tale from the wrong motives may sow the seeds of genuine repentance. Thus, as in life, the good and the bad are mixed here in one individual, as they are in differing measures in all those on the pilgrimage.

SERMONS AND PREACHING

Since *The Pardoner's Tale* takes the form of a sermon – a lively and very entertaining one – we should examine the medieval idea of both sermons and preachers. In the Middle Ages preachers within the fold of the Catholic Church were regarded as the mouthpieces of God.

Christ as preacher and his instructions to his disciples to go out and preach the gospel were obviously the main influence. We should also note that Christ taught through examples or, as we more commonly call them, parables, and each of these has an accompanying statement of the moral lesson embodied in the example. This idea, of a simple story which could convey great truths to the common people, was central to many of the sermons of the Middle Ages, though frequently it was accompanied by learned theological references for the more educated and enlightened of the listeners. The medieval sermon is thus in many ways a continuation of Christ's basic teaching.

The associations with Chaucer's Pardoner become apparent when we consider the medieval concept of what a preacher should really be like. He should be learned, devout and fervent, thus inspiring respect in his listeners and, of course, he must communicate positively. Preaching was regarded by many at the time as a high vocation, prepared for by the ideal combination in the preacher of confession, prayer and learning. Its primary function was 'public instruction in faith and morals', its benefit for the many, its practice open, its aim the purgation of sin and the cleansing of the soul. The Pardoner is thus a parody of a preacher. He is not devout or fervent but opportunistic. His learning is not deep learning, but a series of acquired references calculated to impress. He is not strictly within the Church but outside, a layman with worldly ambitions which are themselves a denial of true humility and faith. *Parody* is the art of mimicking or imitating a particular style in a satirical, humorous or ironic way in order to expose the author or speaker, in the case of the Pardoner the exposure taking the form of revealing his hypocrisy, his lack of any moral or religious substance in his assuming the role of the preacher. *Irony* is the use of humour and sarcasm to imply the opposite of what is being said or written. Chaucer's presentation of the Pardoner is ironic throughout, since he is showing us a man who practises the opposite of what he preaches. This is simply illustrated by the Pardoner's own choice of theme. If money is the root of all evil then the Pardoner is guilty of sin, for his avowed aim is the acquisition of money and goods, and everything he says is directed towards the achievement of that end.

SIN

In considering *The Pardoner's Tale* it is also necessary to say something about sin both from the point of view of the Church and the place held by it in the medieval mind. Sins were categorized very early in the Christian period, but it was not until the fifth century that Pope Gregory the Great was responsible for incorporating them into Catholic theology. Thereafter the concept of the Seven Deadly Sins was a major influence in the Christian world. Originally Pride was regarded as the basis of Wrath, Envy, Avarice, Sloth (idleness), Gluttony and Luxury (lechery, sexual indulgence). These sins are in fact treated at some length in *The Parson's Tale*, and since the Parson is the one of the religious pilgrims obviously most respected, indeed idealized by Chaucer, we can see how important it is to understand the place of sin in the medieval world.

These sins were thought to be responsible for all the other sins of mankind. Each one, from greed to sexual indulgence, represented earthly pleasure, the placing of selfish practices and ends before obedience to God. The original conception of sin makes it the inheritance of all men since the Fall. Eve was tempted through her senses by the devil, but Adam, created by God as superior, put the love of his wife before his love for God. It was a deliberate decision. From this we see that sin occurs both through the senses and through the overcoming of the intellect and will. The first temptation in the garden of Eden is the model for all subsequent temptations in the minds of medieval men, since mankind consists of the children of Adam and is consequently corruptible, liable to sin, a point made strongly in *The Parson's Tale*.

The Pardoner's theme is based on one of the Seven Deadly Sins, that of Avarice, yet he certainly touches on most of the others and is probably guilty of them himself. He emphatically refers to Sloth (which gives rise to drunkenness and gambling), Gluttony and Luxury. Arguably his own Pride in the pursuit of his trade is a sin, while Wrath and Envy are also displayed in the tale of the three revellers. They show unnatural anger when they meet the old man, while after the criticism of the Host the Pardoner himself is too wrathful to speak. Envy is closely allied to Greed, hence the dual plan in which one reveller decides to kill the other two while they in turn are deciding to kill him. It is clearly demonstrable that *The Pardoner's Tale* is therefore an embodiment of the Seven Deadly Sins, something that would be apparent to the audience of pilgrims. The Seven Deadly Sins are obviously interconnected, one giving rise to the others or at least some of the others.

Councils of the Catholic Church had issued instructions in the thirteenth and fourteenth centuries that priests should preach on these sins to their congregations. The Pardoner, though a layman, was therefore carrying out a Church directive, and this adds a further layer of irony when we consider the man and his practices. Books and stories were also produced for the instruction of the laity, and these frequently had recourse to the Sins, which thus had a wide currency. The aim was obvious. Man in his fallen state could only be saved by a recognition of his errors, followed by penitence, confession, the leading of a Christian life in preparation for an after life in heaven as distinct from the damnation of hell. The Sins were thus ever present in the popular imagination. They were deeply impressed by continual reiteration and vivid representation, as we can see from *The Pardoner's Tale*.

CHAUCER'S LANGUAGE

Chaucer's language, known as Middle English, derives from French, Latin and the native Anglo-Saxon language. In Court circles after the Norman Conquest (1066) French was the dominant language in use. Latin was employed in church documents and services while Anglo-Saxon, which had been the spoken medium before the Conquest, was the main language spoken in the country at large and was slowly assimilating aspects of the others. One sees therefore that there are three main influences on Chaucer, and that it is a measure of his genius that he was able to acquire and integrate them. This is what gives his language its richness and variety.

There would be little point here in setting out a table of Chaucerian grammar which could be learned and, with some difficulty, applied to *The Pardoner's Tale* and any other of Chaucer's writings which the student feels moved to read. Chaucer's language is the origin of our own, a development of the London and East Midlands dialect which was gradually becoming the received language. As you read and listen to this language you will become aware of certain basic grammatical forms and usages which are different from those of our own time. For example, you will find in *The Pardoner's Tale* the use of the hyphenated y (y-) to make a past participle, as in y-set (seated), y-spoken (spoken), y-slawe (killed), and y-stonge (stung). The fact that Chaucer was using a developing language, and developing it himself, is seen in his occasional removal of that y, as in y-clepen (called or be called) which he contracts to clepeth in *The Pardoner's Tale*. The rules of grammar were not fixed, and the language became more flexible under Chaucer's guiding hand.

Another interesting usage is that of the negative. When the old man says to the revellers of Death that

> Nat for your boost he wol him no-thing hyde

we translate it as 'he will not hide because of your boast', for the double negative has produced a negative instead of a positive, as in modern English. Read Chaucer's sentences carefully, and the underlying sense is usually apparent.

For the modern reader the vocabulary presents some difficulty. We are faced with words which (a) mean the same, or roughly the same as they do today, (b) words which look as if they mean the same as today, but don't and (c) words which meant something in Chaucer's time but are obsolete in our own. Only close working through the text and checking against the glossary and the notes in this edition will provide you with a sound knowledge of Chaucer's language. Let us examine a few lines from *The Pardoner's Tale* at random:

> He seith, he can no difference finde
> Bitwix a man that is out of his minde
> And a man which that is dronkelewe,
> But that woodnesse, y-fallen in a shrewe,
> Persevereth lenger . . .

Two words, 'woodnesse' and 'shrewe', present difficulty and must be looked up; the first means madness from the old English word 'wod' meaning mad. The second means a wicked or ill-disposed man or person, and here the rendering of 'miserable creature' probably fits best. We have already glanced at the hyphenated y, and we shall find that one of the meanings of 'fallen' is 'befall', or 'occur' in the modern sense; 'dronkelewe' is a finely suggestive word meaning 'habitually drunk', and the rest of the quotation, while it needs checking, is virtually self-evident. Note 'out of his minde', a phrase which is still a commonplace colloquialism for insanity, whether of a serious or, in the opinion of the speaker, a temporary nature. A study of the above quotation, a working out of the complete sense and the piecing together of a meaningful translation, is part and parcel of the good student's approach to Chaucer.

It is essential to read Chaucer in the original to get the feel of the language, and preferably to read it aloud in order to assimilate the sounds of the spoken words so far removed from our own in time. You should listen to a recording or the pronunciation of a good reader if possible; imitate what you hear, reciting some of the lines of *The Pardoner's Tale*, which is written in rhyming couplets. Chaucer's spelling was largely phonetic, and when you read you should aim to pronounce all the letters, including the final 'e' of a word unless it precedes another vowel – and which is said like the second 'e' in 'never'. Take the third and fourth lines of *The Pardoner's Prologue* and notice how the final 'e' before a vowel is not sounded but that those before a consonant or at the end of a line are:

> And ringe it out as round as gooth a belle,
> For I can al by rote that I telle.

Chaucer normally employs a ten-syllable line, but when the final 'e' of a line is pronounced the line has eleven syllables and rhymes with an eleven-syllable line. There is no short cut with Chaucer. Sit down and work through a section at a time – say a verse paragraph – taking care not to do too much at one sitting. This will enable you to get the sound and sense of the language, and will bring its own reward in increased and confident familiarity. You will gradually become aware of Chaucer's technical and imaginative expertise. Take the following two lines from the Tale:

> Allas! the shorte throte, the tendre mouth,
> Maketh that, Est and West, and North and South,

where a variety of vowel sounds and the balancing 'Ts' and 'Ths' almost convey the delicious swallowing of the food, each of the qualified nouns in the first line and the single-word effects in the second reflecting the action.

In summary, what you must do is listen to the text wherever possible, apply yourself closely to it, looking up all words which present difficulty, making sure that you know any obsolete words and checking constantly on exact meanings and changes of meanings. Speak the text after listening to a recording or a good reader, pronouncing all the letters including the final 'e' (unless that 'e' comes before a word beginning with a vowel). We have seen that Chaucer's vowels are often rich in sound, and that the consonants too can contribute to the music of the verse. Some of these consonants – like the 'gh' in 'taughte' and 'draughte' – were pronounced in Chaucer's time and, after you have listened to a reading, you will see that a sound something like our own 'ct' as in 'doctor' is being conveyed. Chaucer's couplets can be quite easily scanned for their ten or eleven syllable content, syllables that you emphasize normally alternating with those you don't, as in:

> Thanne peyne I me to strecche forth the nekke

This is a good example of the eleven syllable line, but don't feel that you have to master the technicalities of verse. Reading aloud and working out the syllabic content will help you to a fuller appreciation of both the sound and the content of Chaucer's poem.

The Text, with Modern Rendering and Notes

This rendering of Chaucer into modern English is not meant to be a crib. As far as possible the original has been put into colloquial English, but where the original is difficult in terms of construction, additional words in brackets have been included to make the *sense* clear. The student reading the Chaucer text should test his own translation against the editor's, using the glossary on page 142 of this Passnote and the notes at the foot of each page of translation. That is the only way to a thorough mastery of this prescribed text.

THE GENERAL PROLOGUE

   With him ther rood a gentil Pardoner
Of Rouncival, his freend and his compeer,
That streight was comen fro the court of Rome.
Ful loude he song, 'Com hider, love, to me.'
This somnour bar to him a stif burdoun,   5
Was never trompe of half so greet a soun.
This pardoner hadde heer as yelow as wex,
But smothe it heng, as dooth a strike of flex;
By ounces henge his lokkes that he hadde,
And ther-with he his shuldres overspradde;   10
But thinne it lay, by colpons oon and oon;
But hood, for Iolitee, ne wered he noon,
For it was trussed up in his walet.
Him thoughte, he rood al of the newe Iet;
Dischevele, save his cappe, he rood al bare.   15
Swiche glaringe eyen hadde he as an hare.

THE PARDONER IN THE GENERAL PROLOGUE

With him (the Summoner) there travelled his close friend the superior Pardoner who was attached to the foundation of Mary of Roncevalles. He had just come from the Papal Court in Rome. He sang loudly 'Come hither, love, to me'. The Summoner sang the refrain by way of accompaniment – never a trumpet or trumpeter sounded half so loud. The Pardoner's hair was as yellow as wax, but it hung as smoothly as a hank of flax. The locks of his hair hung in little bits and were spread over his shoulders in thin wispy single strands. He didn't wear a hood, but carried it folded up in his bag. He thought that he rode in the latest fashion. He rode with his hair hanging loose, apart from his cap. He had staring eyes like a hare.

1   *gentil*: Chaucer is using the word ironically. There is nothing superior or gracious about the Pardoner.
2   *Rouncival*: A 'cell' at Charing Cross of the Priory of St Mary of Roncevalles, the town and the original foundation being in the Pyrenees in France.
4   *'Com hider, love, to me'*: A line from a popular song, the choice of which shows the Pardoner's worldly rather than spiritual concerns.
5   *a stif burdoun*: The refrain of the song, sung in the bass line in this case.
6   *trompe*: Chaucer is again being ironic – both the Summoner and the Pardoner are loud – a measure of their insensitivity, of their 'flawed' natures.
11 *colpons*: Wisps, indicating the unattractive, almost grotesque appearance of the Pardoner.
12 *Iolitee*: Comfort, here ironic because he really doesn't wear the hood – he is intent on displaying his hair.
14 *newe Iet*: Latest fashion, again indicative of his vanity and worldliness.
16 *glaringe eyen . . . as an hare*: Again the description is unattractive but the hare is a symbol of fertility – ironic in view of the Pardoner's lack of sexuality, though his relationship with the Summoner is odd.

A vernicle hadde he sowed on his cappe.
His walet lay biforn him in his lappe,
Bret-ful of pardoun come from Rome al hoot.
A voys he hadde as smal as hath a goot.   20
No berd hadde he, ne never sholde have,
As smothe it was as it were late y-shave;
I trowe he were a gelding or a mare.
But of his craft, fro Berwik into Ware,
Ne was ther swich another pardoner.   25
For in his male he hadde a pilwe-beer,
Which that, he seyde, was our lady veyl:
He seyde, he hadde a gobet of the seyl
That sëynt Peter hadde, whan that he wente
Up-on the see, til Iesu Crist him hente.   30
He hadde a croys of latoun, ful of stones,
And in a glas he hadde pigges bones.
But with thise relikes, whan that he fond
A povre person dwelling up-on lond,
Up-on a day he gat him more moneye   35
Than that the person gat in monthes tweye.

He had sewn a badge of St Veronica on his cap. His wallet lay on his lap in front of him and was crammed with pardons freshly arrived from Rome. He had a voice as feeble as a goat's. He had no beard, and would never have one now, being as smooth as if he had been recently shaved. I think he was a gelding or a mare. But as to his trade, there was no other Pardoner to match him between Berwick and Ware. For in his bag he had a pillow-case which he asserted was the Blessed Virgin Mary's veil. He said that he had a piece of the sail that belonged to St Peter when he walked on the sea of Galilee till Jesus Christ seized him. He had a pinchbeck cross full of stones, as well as pigs' bones in a glass. But with these relics, when he came upon a poor parson living in the countryside, he was able to make more money in one day than that parson was able to earn in two months.

17   *A vernicle*: The word is derived from the name Veronica, for it was St Veronica who wiped Christ's face with her veil on the road to Calvary. The image of his face was miraculously preserved on it, and was kept in St Peter's in Rome. The badge worn by the Pardoner is a souvenir of this.

23   *a gelding or a mare*: A Chaucerian comment implying that the Pardoner is impotent or a eunuch, a physical equivalent to his spiritual impotence.

26–32   *pilwe-beer . . . pigges bones*: The relics of saints are thought to work miracles as well as preserving the welfare of the soul if they are prayed to devoutly. Pardoners were adept at producing faked relics to impress their audiences and to get money from them. Ironically, the purpose of the pilgrimage to Canterbury was to visit a shrine with real relics, those of Thomas à Becket.

28–9   *the seyl/That sëynt Peter hadde*: Another fake – Peter was a fisherman before he was called by Christ to be one of his disciples, so this is sales-talk implying that such a relic would be rare. The calling of Peter is separate – see John 1:42.

34   *person*: 'Parson' not 'person'.

And thus, with feyned flaterye and Iapes,
He made the person and the peple his apes.
But trewely to tellen, atte laste,
He was in chirche a noble ecclesiaste.   40
Wel coude he rede a lessoun or a storie,
But alderbest he song an offertorie;
For wel he wiste, whan that song was songe,
He moste preche, and wel affyle his tonge,
To winne silver, as he ful wel coude;   45
Therefore he song so meriely and loude.

Thus, with insincerity and tricks, he made fools of the parson and his flock. But, finally and truthfully, he was a fine religious officer in Church. He could read superbly a lesson or a saint's legend, but best of all was his rendering of the offertory, for he knew only too well that when the anthem was completed, he would have to preach with a smooth tongue in order to earn as much money as he could. Therefore he sang so cheerfully and loudly.

37–8 *flaterye and Iapes . . . the peple his apes*: Note that these words apply to the Pardoner's method and the measure of his success in *The Pardoner's Tale* itself.

42 *offertorie*: The part of the service at which the members of the congregation offer bread and wine to the priests as gifts. It often led to arguments as to who should go first.

WORDS OF THE HOST

The wordes of the Host to the Phisicien and the Pardoner.

Our Hoste gan to swere as he were wood,
'Harrow!' quod he, 'by nayles and by blood!
This was a fals cherl and a fals Iustyse!
As shamful deeth as herte may devyse
Come to thise Iuges and hir advocats!   5
Algate this sely mayde is slayn, allas!
Allas! to dere boghte she beautee!
Wherfore I seye al day, as men may see,
That yiftes of fortune or of nature
Ben cause of deeth to many a creature.   10
Hir beautee was hir deeth, I dar wel sayn;
Allas! so pitously as she was slayn!
Of bothe yiftes that I speke of now
Men han ful ofte more harm than prow.
But trewely, myn owene mayster dere,   15
This is a pitous tale for to here.
But natheles, passe over, is no fors;
I prey to god, so save thy gentil cors,
And eek thyne urinals and thy Iordanes,
Thyn Ypocras, and eek thy Galianes,   20
And every boist ful of thy letuarie;
God blesse hem, and our lady seinte Marie!
So mot I theen, thou art a propre man,
And lyk a prelat, by seint Ronyan!

THE WORDS OF THE HOST TO THE
PHYSICIAN AND THE PARDONER

Our Host began to swear as if he were mad: 'Alas,' he said, 'by the nails and blood (of Christ on the cross) this was a treacherous villain and a wicked magistrate. The most shameful death which the mind of man can conceive fall upon all such judges and their lawyers! All the same, sadly this innocent girl was slain. Alas, she paid too high a price for being beautiful. This is why I always say, as you may see, that the blessings of fortune or of nature are the causes of many a person's death. Her beauty brought about her death, I have no doubt. Alas, she was killed so piteously. From both the gifts I have just mentioned (fortune and nature) people often derive more harm than good. But truly, my own dear master, this is a very sad tale to have to listen to. Nevertheless, let's forget it, it doesn't matter. I pray to God to preserve your noble body and also your urinals and your chamber-pots too, your spicy-flavoured wine and also your drinks named after Galen, and every box filled with your medicines. God and our Lady St Mary bless them. As I hope to do well for myself, you are a fine man, and just like a bishop, by St Ronyan.

9 *yiftes of fortune or of nature*: Qualities of intelligence and beauty are the gifts of nature, whereas those of fortune are status or rank in society as well as prosperity and wealth.
19 *Iordanes*: Chamber-pots, but the origin is uncertain. It may even have meant a bottle of water brought from the River Jordan.
20 *Ypocras ... Galianes*: Names derived from Hippocrates (?460–?377 B.C.), the Greek physician often called the father of medicine, and Galen (A.D. ?130–?200), Greek medical authority influential right up to the Renaissance.
24 *seint Ronyan*: Possibly an error for St Ninian (d. A.D. 432), the apostle of Christianity in North Britain.

Seyde I nat wel? I can nat speke in terme;   25
But wel I woot, thou doost my herte to erme,
That I almost have caught a cardiacle.
By corpus bones! but I have triacle,
Or elles a draught of moyste and corny ale,
Or but I here anon a mery tale,   30
Myn herte is lost for pitee of this mayde.
Thou bel amy, thou Pardoner,' he seyde,
'Tel us som mirthe or Iapes right anon.'
'It shall be doon,' quod he, 'by seint Ronyon!
But first,' quod he, 'heer at his ale-stake   35
I wol both drinke, and eten of a cake.'
   But right anon thise gentils gonne to crye,
'Nay! lat him telle us of no ribaudye;
Tel us som moral thing, that we may lere
Som wit, and thanne wol we gladly here.'   40
'I graunte, y-wis,' quod he, 'but I mot thinke
Up-on som honest thing, whyl that I drinke.

Didn't I speak well? I can't use your technical terms. But I know only too well that you have moved me so that I have nearly had a heart attack. By God's bones, unless I have some medicine, or else a good drink of fresh strong ale, or unless I straightaway hear a merry story, my heart is overcome with pity for this girl. You, my good fellow, you, Pardoner,' he said, 'now tell us something happy or some jokes.'

'By St Ronyan I will,' he said, 'but first,' he added, 'I'll have a drink and some cake to eat here at this inn-sign.'

But straightaway at this the more refined ones cried out, 'No, don't let him relate anything filthy. Tell us some moral tale so that we may learn some wisdom, and then we'll gladly listen.'

'Certainly I agree,' he said, 'but I must think of some decent subject while I am having a drink.'

28 *By corpus bones*: Note that here as elsewhere in the words of the Host we are being ironically prepared for the blasphemy which is to mark *The Pardoner's Tale*.

32 *bel amy*: The language here is mock courteous, hence the choice of French, the language of the Court.

37 *thise gentils*: In effect a Chaucerian recognition of the (supposed) different moral caste of the classes – refined people naturally preferring something moral, the lower orders something to satisfy their dirty minds.

THE PROLOGUE OF THE PARDONERS TALE

Here folweth the Prologe of the Pardoners Tale.

Radix malorum est Cupiditas: Ad Thimotheum, sexto.

'Lordings,' quod he, 'in chirches whan I preche,
I peyne me to han an hauteyn speche,
And ringe it out as round as gooth a belle,
For I can al by rote that I telle.
My theme is alwey oon, and ever was —   5
"*Radix malorum est Cupiditas.*"
  'First I pronounce whennes that I come,
And than my bulles shewe I, alle and somme.
Our lige lordes seel on my patente,
That shewe I first, my body to warente,   10
That no man be so bold, ne preest ne clerk,
Me to destourbe of Cristes holy werk;

THE PARDONER'S PROLOGUE

'Good people,' he said, 'when I speak in churches, I take the trouble to speak loudly and in an elevated way and ring it out (my sermon) as clearly as the ringing of a bell, for I know everything that I say by heart. My text is always the same and always has been – "for the love of money is the root of all evil".

'First I announce where I have come from, and then I display my Papal bulls – all of them – to each and every one. Before this I display the seal of our Bishop upon my patent in order to protect myself, so that no man, priest nor clerk, could be foolhardy enough to hinder me from carrying out Christ's holy work.

2 *hauteyn*: Loud, resonant, but with the implication of haughtiness, thus emphasizing the Pardoner's affected superiority and the beginning of his 'act'.

6 *'Radix malorum est Cupiditas.'*: 'For the love of money is the root of all evil.' 1 Timothy 6:10. This is the theme of the Pardoner's story, with the accompanying irony that the Pardoner does not practise what he preaches.

7 *whennes that I come*: According to the General Prologue (see line 3 of the first section) the Pardoner has just come from Rome, but this would almost certainly be a boast rather than a fact.

8 *my bulles*: Official documents with the authentic seals attached to them.

9 *lige lordes seel*: The seal of the Bishop who authorized the Pardoner.

10 *body*: His person, meaning that his body will not be subject to attack.

11 *ne preest ne clerk*: They might be inclined to cast doubt on the Pardoner, since they are Churchmen and he is a layman. Another instance of Chaucer's irony.

And after that than telle I forth my tales,
Bulles of popes and of cardinales,
Of patriarkes, and bishoppes I shewe;   15
And in Latyn I speke a wordes fewe,
To saffron with my predicacioun,
And for to stire men to devocioun.
Than shewe I forth my longe cristal stones,
Y-crammed ful of cloutes and of bones;   20
Reliks been they, as wenen they echoon.
Than have I in latoun a sholder-boon
Which that was of an holy Iewes shepe.
"Good men," seye I, "tak of my wordes kepe;
If that this boon be wasshe in any welle,   25
If cow, or calf, or sheep, or oxe swelle
That any worm hath ete, or worm y-stonge,
Tak water of that welle, and wash his tonge,
And it is hool anon; and forthermore,
Of pokkes and of scabbe, and every sore   30
Shal every sheep be hool, that of this welle
Drinketh a draughte; tak kepe eek what I telle.

And after that I proceed to repeat what I have to say. I set forth the bulls of Popes and Cardinals, Patriarchs and Bishops, and I speak a few words in Latin in order to season my preaching and in order to encourage them (my listeners) towards religious fervour. Then I produce my large glass boxes crammed full with rags and bones. All of them believe that these are religious relics. Then I have a shoulder-bone set in latten which came from the sheep of a holy Jew. "Good friends," I say, "mark my words well. If this bone is dipped in any well, and if a cow, calf, sheep or ox that has been eaten or stung by any snake or insect becomes ill then takes water of that well and bathes its tongue, it will quickly recover. Moreover, the various diseases of the skin will be cured in every sheep which drinks from this well. Take note also of what else I have to say.

14 *Bulles of popes* ...: The authentic document having been produced, the Pardoner refers to others which are almost certainly false.
15 *patriarkes*: Leading Churchmen in charge of a group of Archbishops.
17 *To saffron with my predicacioun*: The metaphor is from cooking, the saffron plant being employed (still) to provide colour and taste. The Pardoner is, so to speak, dressing his own dish.
22 *in latoun*: In an alloy, here brass.
23 *holy Iewes shepe*: The Pardoner is being deliberately vague, implying an unnamed but impressively religious biblical figure. The irony lies in the fact that the Jews had been expelled from England.

If that the good-man, that the bestes oweth,
Wol every wike, er that the cok him croweth,
Fastinge, drinken of this welle a draughte,   35
As thilke holy Iewe our eldres taughte,
His bestes and his stoor shal multiplye.
And, sirs, also it heleth Ialousye;
For, though a man be falle in Ialous rage,
Let maken with this water his potage,   40
And never shal he more his wyf mistriste,
Though he the sooth of hir defaute wiste;
Al had she taken preestes two or three.
    ' "Heer is a miteyn eek, that ye may see.
He that his hond wol putte in this miteyn,   45
He shal have multiplying of his greyn,
Whan he hath sowen, be it whete or otes,
So that he offre pens, or elles grotes.
    Good men and wommen, o thing warne I yow,
If any wight be in this chirche now,   50
That hath doon sinne horrible, that he
Dar nat, for shame, of it y-shriven be,
Or any womman, be she yong or old,
That hath y-maad hir housbond cokewold,
Swich folk shul have no power ne no grace   55
To offren to my reliks in this place.

If the good man who owns the animals will, every week, before the cock crows, abstain from eating, drink from this well, as this holy Jew taught our ancestors, his beasts and his livestock shall multiply. And moreover, gentlemen, it also cures sexual jealousy, for although a man has fallen into a jealous fit, if he makes his soup using this water, then he will never again doubt his wife even though he knows the truth of her offence even to her taking (as lovers) two or three priests.

' "Here also is a mitten that you can see. He who puts his hand into this mitten will find that his grain will multiply after he has sown it, no matter if it is wheat or oats, provided that he offers up pence or groats.

' "Good men and women, I warn you of one thing; if there is any man in this church now who has sinned so horribly that he dare not, out of shame, come for forgiveness, or if there is any woman, young or old, who has been unfaithful to her husband – such people shall not be granted the favour of making an offer for my relics in this place.

38 *Ialousye*: Sexual jealousy. Notice that the Pardoner is exploiting to the full the gullibility of his listeners.

43 *Al had she taken preestes two or three*: A sly dig at the unfaithfulness of women and at the promiscuity of priests, topics of interest – gossip – frequently occurring in this period. The remark shows the Pardoner's ability to gauge his audience and *their* interest in common gossip of this kind.

44 *miteyn:* Worn by a farmer when he is sowing seed.

48 *pens . . . grotes*: Pennies . . . silver coins (worth about 4p in today's currency).

52 *y-shriven*: Be exposed (publicly), with the association of confessing one's sins to a priest. As a layman, the Pardoner could not 'hear' private confessions.

54 *cokewold*: Cuckold (from the old French for 'cuckoo'). Notice how the Pardoner is still using moral blackmail by playing on sexual sin.

And who-so findeth him out of swich blame,
He wol com up and offre in goddes name,
And I assoille him by the auctoritee
Which that by bulle y-graunted was to me."   60
  'By this gaude have I wonne, yeer by yeer,
An hundred mark sith I was Pardoner.
I stonde lyk a clerk in my pulpet,
And whan the lewed peple is doun y-set,
I preche, so as ye han herd bifore,   65
And telle an hundred false Iapes more.
Than peyne I me to strecche forth the nekke,
And est and west upon the peple I bekke,
As doth a dowve sitting on a berne.
Myn hondes and my tonge goon so yerne,   70
That it is Ioye to see my bisinesse.
Of avaryce and of swich cursednesse
Is al my preching, for to make hem free
To yeve her pens, and namely un-to me.
For my entente is nat but for to winne,   75
And no-thing for correccioun of sinne.

And whosoever finds himself free from such sin may come up and offer in God's name, and I will absolve him through the authority vested in me by this papal bull."

'I have made a hundred marks a year by this trick since I have been a Pardoner. I stand like an ecclesiastic in my pulpit, and when the common people have sat down, I preach, as you have heard me previously, and tell another hundred falsehoods. Then I take pains to lean my neck far forward, and I nod at the people on all sides of me, like a dove sitting on a barn. My gestures and my words go (together) so briskly that it is pleasure to see me at my work. All my preaching is against avarice and such vices so as to make them give their pennies, generously, to me. For my sole aim is to make a profit and is not at all concerned with the correction of sins.

59 *assoille*: Absolve, again something the Pardoner cannot strictly do. The Church only empowered him to pardon. After absolution (which had to be given by a priest) a sinner still had to work towards repentance. It became common practice to give money, via a pardoner, which would be for the use of the Church. It is clear how the confusion between absolution and pardon occurred in the common mind.

61 *By this gaude*: By this trick. This confession or boast shows that although the Pardoner is a rogue he is willing (at least in this company) to acknowledge it.

62 *An hundred mark*: The boast continues with this reference – unashamed – to an income representing, in Chaucer's time, a very large sum of money. The Pardoner is prosperous.

64 *lewed peple*: Common, ill-educated. Note the Pardoner's condescending tone.

69 *As doth a dowve sitting on a berne*: A simile from country life, indicative of Chaucer's times, where village life and farming would predominate.

71 *it is Ioye to see my bisinesse*: Chaucer's irony is at the Pardoner's obvious self-conceit and delight in his own performance.

75 *to winne*: To make a profit. This boasting undermines all the Pardoner's spiritual pretensions.

I rekke never, whan that they ben beried,
Though that her soules goon a-blakeberied!
For certes, many a predicacioun
Comth ofte tyme of yvel entencioun;   80
Som for plesaunce of folk and flaterye,
To been avaunced by ipocrisye,
And som for veyne glorie, and som for hate.
For, whan I dar non other weyes debate,
Than wol I stinge him with my tonge smerte   85
In preching, so that he shal nat asterte
To been defamed falsly, if that he
Hath trespased to my brethren or to me.
For, though I telle noght his propre name,
Men shal wel knowe that it is the same   90
By signes and by othere circumstances.
Thus quyte I folk that doon us displesances;
Thus spitte I out my venim under hewe
Of holynesse, to seme holy and trewe.

I do not care, after they have been buried, if their souls are to be damned. For it is certain that many a sermon springs often from evil intentions. Some, to please and flatter the people, are promoted by hypocrisy, and some for empty pride, and some for hate. For when I do not dare to preach in other ways, then I will attack someone with my sharp tongue in my preaching so that he will not escape being falsely dishonoured if he has caused harm to me or my associates. For although I do not mention him by name, men will be aware of his identity through my hints and by other means. In this way I repay those who displease us. Thus do I spit out my poison under the appearance of virtue in order to seem pious and truthful.

78 *her soules goon a-blakeberied!*: An instance once more from country life. 'I don't care where their souls go to' is the implication, just as people in search of blackberries go all over the place, perhaps even getting lost in their search.

80 *Comth ofte tyme of yvel entencioun*: Note the irony – the Pardoner's intention *is* evil – he is concerned only with making money.

88 *my brethren*: The Pardoner is speaking as if he and his fellow Pardoners were a genuine religious order. This assumption is calculated to deceive the simple members of his usual audience.

89 *propre*: Own – of course the Pardoner does *not* know, but is cunning enough to blackmail his audience into believing that he does.

93 *Thus spitte I out my venim ...*: Another image from nature – here the Pardoner is comparing himself to a snake – with the contrast of virtue and venom effectively demonstrating the hypocrisy of the Pardoner. He *appears* virtuous but is in fact *venomous*, for he is *poisoning* true religion. His motive is *revenge*, and the snake image suggests the Devil.

'But shortly myn entente I wol devyse;   95
I preche of no-thing but for coveityse.
Therfor my theme is yet, and ever was –
"Radix malorum est cupiditas."
Thus can I preche agayn that same vyce
Which that I use, and that is avaryce.   100
But, though my-self be gilty in that sinne
Yet can I maken other folk to twinne
From avaryce, and sore to repente.
But that is nat my principal entente.
I preche no-thing but for coveityse;   105
Of this matere it oughte y-nogh suffyse.
    'Than telle I hem ensamples many oon
Of olde stories, longe tyme agoon:
For lewed peple loven tales olde;
Swich thinges can they wel reporte and holde.   110
What? trowe ye, the whyles I may preche,
And winne gold and silver for I teche,
That I wol live in povert wilfully?
Nay, nay, I thoghte it never trewely!
For I wol preche and begge in sondry londes;   115
I wol not do no labour with myn hondes,
Ne make baskettes, and live therby,
Because I wol nat beggen ydelly.

'But I will shortly outline my intentions. I preach for nothing but greed, and therefore my text is still and always has been that "for the love of money is the root of evil" (*Radix malorum est cupiditas*). In this way I can preach against the one vice which I practise, namely that of avarice. But although I myself am guilty of that sin, yet I can make other people reject avarice and repent deeply. But that is not my main motive. I only preach from my own greed. That should be enough on this subject.

'Then I tell them illustrative tales, many from old stories set in the distant past, for ignorant people love old stories; such things they can easily remember and talk about. What! do you think that while I may preach and earn gold and silver from my teachings, that I will deliberately live in poverty? No, no, I never really believed that! For I will preach and beg in various lands, I will not do manual work, nor make baskets and earn a living in that way, for I will not beg in vain.

95 *But shortly myn entente I wol devyse*: The Pardoner does just this, for any audience he spoke to would not have copies of what he was saying!

107 *ensamples*: Technical term for the illustrative stories which support the main argument in a medieval sermon, which is what *The Pardoner's Tale* is.

117 *Ne make baskettes*: Perhaps Chaucer or more probably the Pardoner is confusing St Paul the Apostle with the little known St Paul the Hermit, whose trade was basket-making.

I wol non of the apostles counterfete;
I wol have money, wolle, chese, and whete,   120
Al were it yeven of the povrest page,
Or of the povrest widwe in a village,
Al sholde hir children sterve for famyne.
Nay! I wol drinke licour of the vyne,
And have a Ioly wenche in every toun.   125
But herkneth, lordings, in conclusioun;
Your lyking is that I shal telle a tale.
Now, have I dronke a draughte of corny ale,
By god, I hope I shal yow telle a thing
That shal, by resoun, been at your lyking.   130
For, though myself be a ful vicious man,
A moral tale yet I yow telle can,
Which I am wont to preche, for to winne.
Now holde your pees, my tale I wol beginne.'

I will not imitate any of the apostles. I will have money, wool, cheese and wheat, even if it is taken from the poorest serving-boy or from the poorest village widow, even if it means that her children die of hunger. No! I will drink wine, and have a pretty girl in every town. But listen (ladies and) gentlemen, in conclusion. Your wish is that I shall tell a story. Now that I have drunk some strong ale, by God I hope that I shall tell you something to your liking if you are reasonable. For although I myself am a very unprincipled man, I can still tell you a moral tale of the kind that I usually preach for profit. Now be quiet – I will begin my story.'

119 *non of the apostles counterfete*: This underlines the confusion above – the Pardoner would not imitate an Apostle engaged in menial work.

123 *Al sholde hir children sterve for famyne . . .*: There is a shameless self-honesty about the Pardoner here, exemplified in the following lines which indulge the good things of life with lip-smacking enjoyment. It is important to remember that sex and other forms of self-indulgence are encompassed in 'cupiditas', so that the Pardoner is revealing himself for what he really is.

131 *though myself be a ful vicious man*: The irony lies in the fact that such a man can tell a moral tale, and yet have no intention of leading a moral life, but can convert others.

THE PARDONERS TALE

Here biginneth the Pardoners Tale.

In Flaundres whylom was a companye   135
Of yonge folk, that haunteden folye,
As ryot, hasard, stewes, and tavernes,
Wher-as, with harpes, lutes, and giternes,
They daunce and pleye at dees bothe day and night,
And ete also and drinken over hir might,   140
Thurgh which they doon the devel sacrifyse
With-in that develes temple, in cursed wyse,
By superfluitee abhominable;
Hir othes been so grete and so dampnable,
That it is grisly for to here hem swere;   145
Our blissed lordes body they to-tere;
Hem thoughte Iewes rente him noght y-nough;
And ech of hem at otheres sinne lough.

THE PARDONER'S TALE

Once upon a time in Flanders there was a group of young people who behaved sinfully, (living) riotously, gambling, (visiting) brothels and taverns, while with harps, lutes and stringed instruments, they danced and played with dice both day and night. They also ate and drank more than they should have done, and in so doing they made sacrifice to the Devil within the Devil's own temple (the tavern) in this accursed manner through their abominable excesses. Their oaths were so strong and so merited damnation that it was offensive to hear them swear. They tear our blessed Lord's body, it seeming to them that the Jews had not wounded him enough, and each of them laughed at the sins of the others.

135 *In Flaundres whylom*: This is deliberately set in a vague past, though it might have some contemporary bite – Flanders was associated with drunkenness and in Chaucer's time Flemish settlers in England were not welcomed.

137 *hasard*: The general term for gambling as well as the gamble in which the thrower guesses the number before he throws the dice.

138 *giternes*: Like the lutes, these were stringed instruments in some ways equivalent to modern guitars.

141 *the devel sacrifyse/With-in that develes temple*: This idea of the tavern being the devil's church is an ironic one, the forms of worship being the sins of gluttony, drinking, swearing, gambling and whoring.

146 *Our blissed lordes body they to-tere*: Verbal blasphemy of this kind in Chaucer's time was attacked by the Church, which saw every oath as a re-crucifying of Christ.

147 *Hem thoughte Iewes*: This reflects the anti-Semitism of this period and succeeding periods, the Jews being blamed for the murder of Christ. They were persecuted, isolated, and expelled from England by two major edicts in 1290 and 1306.

And right anon than comen tombesteres
Fetys and smale, and yonge fruytesteres,   150
Singers with harpes, baudes, wafereres,
Whiche been the verray develes officeres
To kindle and blowe the fyr of lecherye,
That is annexed un-to glotonye;
The holy writ take I to my witnesse,   155
That luxurie is in wyn and dronkenesse.
  Lo, how that dronken Loth, unkindely,
Lay by his doghtres two, unwitingly;
So dronke he was, he niste what he wroghte.
  Herodes, (who-so wel the stories soghte),   160
Whan he of wyn was replet at his feste,
Right at his owene table he yaf his heste
To sleen the Baptist Iohn ful giltelees.

And quickly dancing girls would come, graceful and small, and young fruit-sellers, singers with harps, pimps, cake-sellers, all of whom are the real servants of the devil, kindling and blowing the fire of lechery which is linked with gluttony. I refer to the Holy writings for my evidence that wine and drunkenness breed lust.

Look at the way in which the drunken Lot unnaturally but unknowingly slept with his two daughters; he was so drunk that he didn't know what he was doing.

Herod, as those who have read the stories know, when he was full of wine at his feast, gave the command from his own table to kill the completely innocent John the Baptist.

155   *The holy writ ... That luxurie is in wyn and dronkenesse*: A convenient interpretation of a statement in St Paul's Epistle to the Ephesians, 5:18 – 'And be not drunk with wine, wherein is excess'. The Pardoner, as we see from the lines which follow, sees excess as sexual licence. He is already observing the form of the medieval sermon, which cites biblical authority in support of a statement.

157   *dronken Loth*: See Genesis 19:30–36. Lot's daughters, mindful of the shortage of men and desiring children, slept with their father on successive nights after they had made him drunk.

160–61   *Herodes ... Whan he of wyn was replet ...*: See Matthew 14:6–10 and Mark 6:21–8. But again the Pardoner is not accurate; neither of these actually says that Herod was drunk, only that he was at a feast. Once more he is using the Bible to impress his audience.

Senek seith eek a good word doutelees;
He seith, he can no difference finde   165
Bitwix a man that is out of his minde
And a man which that is dronkelewe,
But that woodnesse, y-fallen in a shrewe,
Persevereth lenger than doth dronkenesse.
O glotonye, ful of cursednesse,   170
O cause first of our confusioun,
O original of our dampnacioun,
Til Crist had boght us with his blood agayn!
Lo, how dere, shortly for to sayn,
Aboght was thilke cursed vileinye;   175
Corrupt was al this world for glotonye!
Adam our fader, and his wyf also,
Fro Paradys to labour and to wo
Were driven for that vyce, it is no drede;
For whyl that Adam fasted, as I rede,   180
He was in Paradys; and whan that he
Eet of the fruyt defended on the tree,
Anon he was out-cast to wo and peyne.
O glotonye, on thee wel oghte us pleyne!
O, wiste a man how many maladyes   185
Folwen of excesse and of glotonyes,
He wolde been the more mesurable
Of his diete, sittinge at his table.

Seneca's words also are undoubtedly of value; he says that he can find no difference between a man who is out of his mind and a man who is drunk, except that madness, when it has afflicted a wretch, remains with one longer than drunkenness. O gluttony, full of sin, O prime cause of our ruin, O origin of our damnation, until Christ redeemed us again with his blood! To put it briefly, look how dearly this accursed villainy was paid for – this whole world was corrupted by gluttony!

Adam, our father, and his wife too, were driven out of Paradise to labour and suffer for that sin, of that there is no doubt. For as long as Adam abstained from food, so I have read, he was in Paradise. But once he ate of the fruit of the forbidden tree, then forthwith he was cast out to misery and suffering. O gluttony, indeed we ought to complain against you! O, if a man knew how many illnesses are the result of excesses and gluttony, he would take greater care with his diet as he sits at table.

164   *Senek*: Seneca (?4 B.C.–A.D. 65) was the Roman Stoic philosopher, dramatist and adviser to Nero. In one of his letters he calls drunkenness a self-induced madness. The Pardoner is virtually correct here!

170   *O glotonye . . .*: Note the rhetorical exclamation (O) which is repeated and which is calculated to arouse emotions – particularly guilt – in the audience. The Pardoner is adept at using the medieval preacher's technique of balancing the authoritative examples with the direct emotional invocation.

177   *Adam our fader . . .*: The idea that Adam's sin in eating of the forbidden fruit was one of gluttony derives from the writing of the Christian monk and scholar St Jerome (A.D. ?347–?420).

182   *the fruyt defended*: Forbidden, the same meaning as its French equivalent now.

Allas! the shorte throte, the tendre mouth,
Maketh that, Est and West, and North and South,   190
In erthe, in eir, in water men to-swinke
To gete a glotoun deyntee mete and drinke!
Of this matere, o Paul, wel canstow trete,
'Mete un-to wombe, and wombe eek un-to mete,
Shal god destroyen bothe,' as Paulus seith.   195
Allas! a foul thing is it, by my feith,
To seye this word, and fouler is the dede,
Whan man so drinketh of the whyte and rede,
That of his throte he maketh his privee,
Thurgh thilke cursed superfluitee.   200
    The apostel weping seith ful pitously,
'Ther walken many of whiche yow told have I,
I seye it now weping with pitous voys,
That they been enemys of Cristes croys,
Of whiche the ende is deeth, wombe is her god.'   205
O wombe! O bely! O stinking cod,
Fulfild of donge and of corrupcioun!
At either ende of thee foul is the soun.
How greet labour and cost is thee to finde!
Thise cokes, how they stampe, and streyne, and grinde,   210

Alas, the small throat and tender mouth ensure that men toil in the four corners of the earth, in earth, air and water to provide delicate meat and drink for the glutton. On this subject, O Paul, you teach well: 'meat into the stomach, and the stomach then into meat, God shall destroy both,' as St Paul said. Alas, by my faith it is a foul thing to talk of this subject, and the deed is fouler, when a man drinks red and white wines like this so that he makes a latrine of his throat through this same damnable excess.

The apostle, in tears, said with great compassion, 'there are many people about such as I have described, I say it now with tears and a pitying tone, that they have been the enemies of Christ and the cross, their stomach is their God and their end will be death.' O stomach, O belly, O stinking bag overfull of muck and corruption! At each end of you there is a foul noise. How great is the labour and the cost to provide for you! These cooks, they stamp and strain and grind

189   *the short throte, the tendre mouth*: The Pardoner's language here, simple and attractive, cunningly conveys the *passing* pleasure as distinct from the *repugnant* aspects of gluttony on which he is to dwell in the lines which follow.

193–5   *Paul . . . as Paulus seith*: From St Paul's First Epistle to the Corinthians, 6:13: 'Meats for the belly, and the belly for meats: but God shall destroy both it and them.'

201   *The apostel*: St Paul once again cited as the Pardoner's authority, in his Epistle to the Philippians, 3:18–19, 'For many walk of whom I have told you often, and now tell you even weeping, that they are the enemies of the cross of Christ: Whose end is destruction, whose God is their belly'.

210   *streyne*: Perhaps with a deliberate pun meaning (a) work to their utmost in terms of physical labour (and imagination) and (b) pass ingredients through strainers in order to extract the essential qualities.

And turnen substaunce in-to accident,
To fulfille al thy likerous talent!
Out of the harde bones knokke they
The mary, for they caste noght a-wey
That may go thurgh the golet softe and swote;   215
Of spicerye, of leef, and bark, and rote
Shal been his sauce y-maked by delyt,
To make him yet a newer appetyt.
But certes, he that haunteth swich delyces
Is deed, whyl that he liveth in tho vyces.   220
    A lecherous thing is wyn, and dronkenesse
Is ful of stryving and of wrecchednesse.
O dronke man, disfigured is thy face,
Sour is thy breeth, foul artow to embrace,

and turn their ingredients into something unrecognizable to satisfy all your greedy inclination. They knock the marrow out of the hard bones, for they don't waste anything that can pass softly and smoothly through the gullet. (The glutton's) sauce shall be made from spices, leaves, barks and roots for his delight to continually renew his appetite. But assuredly he who lives for such delicacies is dead even while he is indulging these vices.

Wine is a lecherous thing, and drunkenness is full of quarrelling and wretchedness. O drunkard, your face is disfigured, your breath is foul, you are loathsome to embrace,

211 *And turnen substaunce in-to accident*: Chaucer, through the Pardoner, is deliberately using, perhaps mocking, medieval philosophical language: *accidents* are the outsides, or appearances, *substaunce* the inside, the essential qualities. Cooks transform the appearance or outside appearance so that we cannot tell what the dish consists of. In the Catholic Mass bread and wine symbolize Christ's body and blood; though they are still *outwardly* bread and wine, the sacrament changes their substance. Thus gluttony is represented here as a blasphemy, or a parody of the spiritual. Compare this to the way in which, at the end of the Tale, two of the rioters gluttonously drink the poisoned wine. The appearance of the wine suggests pleasure but its *substaunce* has been changed. It kills them. When the *substaunce* of wine is changed at the Communion, it offers everlasting life.

215 *softe and swote*: Note how the alliterative 's' and 't' convey the easy sliding and swallowing of food.

219 *But certes . . .*: Another reference to St Paul, this time from the First Epistle to Timothy, 5:6: The widow 'that liveth in pleasure is dead while she liveth'.

And thurgh thy dronke nose semeth the soun   225
As though thou seydest ay 'Sampsoun, Sampsoun';
And yet, god wot, Sampsoun drank never no wyn.
Thou fallest, as it were a stiked swyn;
Thy tonge is lost, and al thyn honest cure;
For dronkenesse is verray sepulture   230
Of mannes wit and his discrecioun.
In whom that drinke hath dominacioun,
He can no conseil kepe, it is no drede.
Now kepe yow fro the whyte and fro the rede,
And namely fro the whyte wyn of Lepe,   235
That is to selle in Fish-strete or in Chepe.
This wyn of Spayne crepeth subtilly
In othere wynes, growing faste by,
Of which ther ryseth swich fumositee,
That whan a man hath dronken draughtes three,   240
And weneth that he be at hoom in Chepe,
He is in Spayne, right at the toune of Lepe,
Nat at the Rochel, ne at Burdeux toun;
And thanne wol he seye, 'Sampsoun, Sampsoun.'

and through your drunken nose comes the sound as though you were always saying 'Samson, Samson'. And yet, God knows, Samson didn't drink wine. You fall down like a stuck pig. You have lost your tongue and all your concern for honourable things, for drunkenness is the very tomb of man's sense and his discretion. The man over whom drink has dominance can certainly keep no secrets. Now keep yourself away from the white and red wines and particularly from the white wine of Lepe which is sold in Fish Street or Cheapside. This Spanish wine finds its way subtly into other wines which are being grown close by, from which mixture there rises such fumes that when a man has had three measures and thinks that he is at home in Cheapside, he is in Spain, right there in the town of Lepe, not at La Rochelle, or the town of Bordeaux. And then he will say, 'Samson, Samson'.

226   *Sampsoun*: The word is onomatopoeic, conveying the heavy breathing through the nose which sounds like the pronunciation of the word. Samson, the biblical giant who epitomizes strength (and who drank no wine), ironically provides the sound and the moral.

236   *Fish-strete or in Chepe*: Main shopping areas in medieval London near which (in Thames Street) Chaucer's father, a wine-merchant, lived.

237   *This wyn of Spayne . . .*: French and Spanish wines were mixed for profit, the more expensive French wines being watered down by the cheaper Spanish wine. The Pardoner is ironically suggesting that they were grown near each other, a deliberate mockery of the malpractice.

239   *fumositee*: Vapours produced by the stomach which affected one's head, according to medieval medical theory.

243   *Rochel . . . Burdeux*: La Rochelle and Bordeaux were centres of the French wine-making trade.

But herkneth, lordings, o word, I yow preye,   245
That alle the sovereyn actes, dar I seye,
Of victories in the olde testament,
Thurgh verray god, that is omnipotent,
Were doon in abstinence and in preyere;
Loketh the Bible, and ther ye may it lere.   250
 Loke, Attila, the grete conquerour,
Deyde in his sleep, with shame and dishonour,
Bledinge ay at his nose in dronkenesse;
A capitayn shoulde live in sobrenesse.
And over al this, avyseth yow right wel   255
What was comaunded un-to Lamuel –
Nat Samuel, but Lamuel, seye I –
Redeth the Bible, and finde it expresly
Of wyn-yeving to hem that han Iustyse.
Na-more of this, for it may wel suffyse.   260
 And now that I have spoke of glotonye,
Now wol I yow defenden hasardrye.
Hasard is verray moder of lesinges,
And of deceite, and cursed forsweringes,
Blaspheme of Crist, manslaughtre, and wast also   265
Of catel and of tyme; and forthermo,
It is repreve and contrarie of honour
For to ben holde a commune hasardour.
And ever the hyër he is of estaat,
The more is he holden desolaat.   270
If that a prince useth hasardrye,
In alle governaunce and policye
He is, as by commune opinioun,
Y-holde the lasse in reputacioun.

But listen, (ladies and) gentlemen, one word I beg you; I have no doubt that all the greatest stories of victories in the Old Testament were achieved through abstinence and prayer, through the true God who is all-powerful. Look in the Bible, and you will find it there.

Look at Attila, the great conqueror, dead in his sleep, with shame and dishonour, bleeding all the time from his nose in his drunken stupor. A commander should live in a sober manner. And above all this, consider fully what was commanded to Lemuel – not Samuel, but Lemuel, I say – read the Bible and find exactly what is said about giving wine to those who have (the dispensing of) justice. No more of this, for it should be enough.

And now that I have spoken of gluttony, I will forthwith forbid you to gamble. Gambling is the very mother of deception, and of trickery and a damnable perjury, of blasphemy against Christ, of killing as well as being a waste of goods and time. And furthermore it is disgraceful and dishonourable to be known as a common gambler. Moreover, the greater is his (the gambler's) status, the greater is his disgrace. If a prince employs gambling throughout all government and administration, his reputation suffers a decline in popular opinion.

251 *Loke, Attila*: The next example, introduced by the familiar 'Look', does not deal with a character from the Bible at all. Attila (A.D. ?406–53), the notorious leader of the Huns who laid waste to much of the Roman Empire, died after a drunken orgy on his wedding night. Hardly a biblical reference, just an example of the Pardoner using any known anecdote to reinforce his arguments.

256 *Lamuel*: See Proverbs 31:4–5, 'It is not for kings, O Lemuel, it is not for kings to drink wine; nor for princes strong drink: Lest they drink, and forget the law, and pervert the judgment of any of the afflicted.'

Stilbon, that was a wys embassadour,   275
Was sent to Corinthe, in ful greet honour,
Fro Lacidomie, to make hir alliaunce.
And whan he cam, him happede, par chaunce,
That alle the grettest that were of that lond,
Pleyinge atte hasard he hem fond.   280
For which, as sone as it mighte be,
He stal him hoom agayn to his contree,
And seyde, 'ther wol I nat lese my name;
Ne I wol nat take on me so greet defame,
Yow for to allye un-to none hasardours.   285
Sendeth othere wyse embassadours;
For, by my trouthe, me were lever dye,
Than I yow sholde to hasardours allye.
For ye that been so glorious in honours
Shul nat allyen yow with hasardours   290
As by my wil, ne as by my tretee.'
This wyse philosophre thus seyde he.

   Loke eek that, to the king Demetrius
The king of Parthes, as the book seith us,
Sente him a paire of dees of gold in scorn,   295
For he hadde used hasard ther-biforn;
For which he heeld his glorie or his renoun
At no value or reputacioun.
Lordes may finden other maner pley
Honeste y-nough to dryve the day awey.   300

Stilbon, who was a wise ambassador, was sent to Corinth from Sparta with great honour to conclude an alliance (with the Co-rinthians). And when he arrived he happened by chance to discover that all the great men of that land were occupied in gambling. Because of this, as soon as possible, he stole back home again to his own country, saying, 'I will not lose my good name there, nor will I take on such a great dishonour by allying you with any gamblers. Send other wise ambassadors for, on my oath, I would die rather than make an alliance for you with gamblers. For you, who have been so honourably glorious, shall not ally yourself with gamblers through my desire nor through my treaty.' Thus spoke this wise philosopher.

Look too at King Demetrius. The King of the Parthians, so we are told in the book, scornfully sent him a pair of golden dice which he had previously used in gambling. Because of this he held his glory and renown to be of no value or estimation. Lords may find other diversions which are decent enough to while away the time.

275 *Stilbon*: This example illustrative of the evils of gambling is found in the story of the ambassador, named Chilon, in the work of John of Salisbury, a twelfth-century writer. Corinth and Sparta (Lacidomie) are two of the Greek city states. The change of subject to gambling indicates a world governed by chance rather than Providence.

293 *the king Demetrius/The king of Parthes*: The Parthians originated from a country in Asia and became a great empire in the second century B.C. It is not clear which King Demetrius is meant, but the story is found in the 'book', the *Policraticus* of John of Salisbury from which Chaucer took the previous example.

Now wol I speke of othes false and grete
A word or two, as olde bokes trete.
Gret swering is a thing abhominable,
And false swering is yet more reprevable.
The heighe god forbad swering at al,   305
Witnesse on Mathew; but in special
Of swering seith the holy Ieremye,
'Thou shalt seye sooth thyn othes, and nat lye,
And swere in dome, and eek in rightwisnesse;'
But ydel swering is a cursednesse.   310
Bihold and see, that in the firste table
Of heighe goddes hestes honurable,
How that the seconde heste of him is this –
'Tak nat my name in ydel or amis.'
Lo, rather he forbedeth swich swering   315
Than homicyde or many a cursed thing;
I seye that, as by ordre, thus it stondeth;
This knowen, that his hestes understondeth,
How that the second heste of god is that.
And forther over, I wol thee telle al plat,   320

Now I will speak a few words of false and great oaths as the old books deal with them. Much swearing is a damnable thing, and swearing false oaths is even more greatly to be condemned. Almighty God forbade all swearing – look at Matthew for evidence. The pious Jeremiah particularly observed on the subject of swearing 'You shall say your oaths truly and not lie, but swear in judgement and in righteousness.' But casual swearing is a great sin. Behold and see that on the first tablet of Almighty God's honourable commandments, note that the second commandment is this – 'Do not take my name idly or wrongly'. Look how he preferred to forbid such swearing before murder or any other sinful act – I say that because of the order in which they (the commandments) are set down. Those who understand the commandments know with what God's second commandment is concerned. And furthermore, I will plainly tell you

306 *Witnesse on Mathew*: See Matthew 5:33–4, 'Again, ye have heard that it hath been said by them of old time, Thou shalt not forswear thyself, but shalt perform unto the Lord thine oaths: But I say unto you, Swear not at all.' This marks the change of subject to swearing, i.e. verbal blasphemy.

307 *the holy Ieremye*: Jeremiah 4:2, 'And thou shalt swear, the Lord liveth, in truth, in judgment, and in righteousness.' Notice that the Pardoner is increasingly citing the weight of biblical authority as he proceeds.

311 *the firste table*: The first five of the Ten Commandments, given by God to Moses on the two tablets of stone on Mount Sinai (Exodus 20).

313 *the seconde heste*: This second commandment (Roman Catholic numbering) against swearing. It would be on the first tablet – 'Thou shall not take the name of the Lord thy God in vain; for the Lord will not hold him guiltless that taketh his name in vain.'

317 *as by ordre*: Swearing comes before murder in the commandments. The Pardoner, typically, is suggesting that it is more important.

That vengeance shal nat parten from his hous,
That of his othes is to outrageous.
'By goddes precious herte, and by his nayles,
And by the blode of Crist, that it is in Hayles,
Seven is my chaunce, and thyn is cink and treye;   325
By goddes armes, if thou falsly pleye,
This dagger shal thurgh-out thyn herte go' –
This fruyt cometh of the bicched bones two,
Forswering, ire, falsnesse, homicyde.
Now, for the love of Crist that for us dyde,   330
Leveth your othes, bothe grete and smale;
But, sirs, now wol I telle forth my tale.

Thise ryotoures three, of whiche I telle,
Longe erst er pryme rong of any belle,
Were set hem in a taverne for to drinke;   335
And as they satte, they herde a belle clinke
Biforn a cors, was caried to his grave;
That oon of hem gan callen to his knave,
'Go bet,' quod he, 'and axe redily,
What cors is this that passeth heer forby;   340
And look that thou reporte his name wel.'

that vengeance will be visited on the house of the man whose oaths are as outrageous as 'By God's precious heart, and by his nails, and by the blood of Christ which is in Hales, seven is my number and yours is five and three'. 'By God's arms, if you cheat, this dagger will go through your heart.' Such results come from the two accursed dice – false oaths, anger, lying, murder. Now, for the love of Christ who died for us, abandon your oaths both great and small. But (ladies and) gentlemen, now I will tell my story.

These three riotous men of whom I speak, long before the first bell had rung, were sitting down to drink in a tavern, and as they sat there they heard a bell chiming in front of a corpse which was being carried to its grave. Then one of them called to his servant, 'Go at once,' he said, 'and quickly ask whose body this is that passes close by us, and make sure that you repeat his name correctly.'

321 *That vengeance shal nat parten from his hous*: Another supportive reference, this to the Apocrypha, here Ecclesiasticus 23:11, 'If he swear in vain, he shall not be innocent, but his house shall be full of calamities.'

324 *the blode of Crist, that it is in Hayles*: A reference to the Abbey of Hales in Gloucestershire which was supposed to have a 'relic' containing Christ's blood.

325 *chaunce*: In the gambling of Chaucer's time, 'chaunce' was a throw of the dice which did not win or lose but which enabled the thrower to have another throw.

325 *cink and treye*: French numbers (compare with the modern French *cinq* and *trois*, or five and three) were used for the six faces of the dice in Chaucer's time.

333 *now wol I telle forth my tale*: The actual tale begins about 200 lines after the Pardoner began speaking, all the examples being calculated to stir his listeners *before* the story.

334 *pryme*: One of the seven times (canonical hours) devoted to prayer in the Church, here six in the morning.

'Sir,' quod this boy, 'it nedeth never-a-del.
It was me told, er ye cam heer, two houres;
He was, pardee, an old felawe of youres;
And sodeynly he was y-slayn to-night,   345
For-dronke, as he sat on his bench upright;
Ther cam a privee theef, men clepeth Deeth,
That in this contree al the peple sleeth,
And with his spere he smoot his herte a-two,
And wente his wey with-outen wordes mo.   350
He hath a thousand slayn this pestilence:
And, maister, er ye come in his presence,
Me thinketh that it were necessarie
For to be war of swich an adversarie:
Beth redy for to mete him evermore.   355
Thus taughte me my dame, I sey na-more.'
'By seinte Marie,' seyde this taverner,
'The child seith sooth, for he hath slayn this yeer,
Henne over a myle, with-in a greet village,
Both man and womman, child and hyne, and page.   360
I trowe his habitacioun be there;
To been avysed greet wisdom it were,
Er that he dide a man a dishonour.'

'Sir,' said the boy, 'it is not necessary. It was told to me two hours before you arrived. It was, in truth, a former mate of yours; he died suddenly last night, dead drunk as he was sitting upright in his seat. There came the secret thief whom men call Death; he kills all the people in this country, and with his spear he burst his (your mate's) heart in two, then went on his way without a word. He has killed a thousand during this plague and, master, before you meet him face to face, I think it is necessary for you to be wary of this foe. Be ready to meet him from now on. Thus my mother taught me; I will say no more.'

'By St Mary,' said this publican, 'the child speaks the truth, for this year he has killed, in a great village over a mile from here, both men, women, children, labourers and servants. I am sure that he lives there. It would be very wise to be prepared before he subjected someone to indignity.'

347–9 *clepeth Deeth . . . And with his spere*: Note the personification of Death which is both visual and vivid. In medieval times Death was sometimes portrayed as a skeleton carrying a spear.

351 *this pestilence*: The frequency of plague and the widespread desolation it caused in the Middle Ages is reflected in the almost casual reference to this particular epidemic.

'Ye, goddes armes,' quod this ryotour,
'Is it swich peril with him for to mete?   365
I shal him seke by wey and eek by strete,
I make avow to goddes digne bones!
Herkneth, felawes, we three been al ones;
Lat ech of us holde up his hond til other,
And ech of us bicomen otheres brother,   370
And we wol sleen this false traytour Deeth;
He shal be slayn, which that so many sleeth,
By goddes dignitee, er it be night.'
   Togidres han thise three her trouthes plight,
To live and dyen ech of hem for other,   375
As though he were his owene y-boren brother.
And up they sterte al dronken, in this rage,
And forth they goon towardes that village,
Of which the taverner had spoke biforn,
And many a grisly ooth than han they sworn,   380
And Cristes blessed body they to-rente –
'Deeth shal be deed, if that they may him hente.'

'Yes, by God's arms,' exclaimed this reveller. 'Is it so dangerous to encounter him? I shall seek him throughout the country, I swear by the noble bones of God. Listen, friends, we three are all together; let each of us raise our hands to each other, and each become the other's brother, and we will kill this false traitor Death. He who has killed so many shall himself be killed, before nightfall, through the nobleness of God.'

Together these three thus swore their oaths, to live and die for each other as though they were brothers from birth. And up they all got in this drunken rage, and set out towards that village of which the publican had previously spoken. And they swore many a hideous oath, and tore Christ's blessed body – 'Death would be dead if they could but take him.'

364 '*Ye, goddes armes*': The swearing much condemned by the Pardoner begins here and characterizes the revellers from now on.

369 *Lat ech of us holde up his hond*: This signifies the oath of blood brotherhood – this swearing is sinful since it foreshadows not betrayal of God but betrayal of man by man.

377 *al dronken*: Notice the care that the Pardoner takes with the structure of his tale – the stress on drunkenness here emphasizes its effect, exemplifying his earlier preaching on its sinfulness.

381 *And Cristes blessed body they to-rente*: Note again the emphatic reference back to his earlier preaching.

382 '*Deeth shal be deed . . .*': The irony lies in the fact that Christ is torn on the Cross but overcomes 'Death' – no amount of blasphemy from man can prevent him from meeting 'Death'.

Whan they han goon nat fully half a myle,
Right as they wolde han troden over a style,
An old man and a povre with hem mette.   385
This olde man ful mekely hem grette,
And seyde thus, 'now, lordes, god yow see!'
  The proudest of thise ryotoures three
Answerde agayn, 'what? carl, with sory grace,
Why artow al forwrapped save thy face?   390
Why livestow so longe in so greet age?'
  This olde man gan loke in his visage,
And seyde thus, 'for I ne can nat finde
A man, though that I walked in-to Inde,
Neither in citee nor in no village,   395
That wolde chaunge his youthe for myn age;
And therfore moot I han myn age stille,
As longe time as it is goddes wille.
  Ne deeth, allas! ne wol nat han my lyf;
Thus walke I, lyk a restelees caityf,   400
And on the ground, which is my modres gate,
I knokke with my staf, bothe erly and late,
And seye, "leve moder, leet me in!
Lo, how I vanish, flesh, and blood, and skin!
Allas! whan shul my bones been at reste?   405
Moder, with yow wolde I chaunge my cheste,
That in my chambre longe tyme hath be,
Ye! for an heyre clout to wrappe me!"
But yet to me she wol nat do that grace,
For which ful pale and welked is my face.   410

When they had gone almost half a mile, just as they were about to climb over a stile, they met a poor old man. This old man greeted them with due politeness, and said, 'Now, lords, God be with you.'

The most arrogant of the three revellers answered back, 'What, churl, bad luck on you! Why are you so tightly wrapped up apart from your face? Why have you lived so long to such a great age?'

This old man looked him in the face and said, 'Because, even if I walked all the way to India, I cannot find a man, neither in a town nor a village, who would exchange his youth for my age. And therefore I must keep my age as long as God wills it.

'Nor will Death, alas, accept my life. Thus I walk on, a wandering wretch, and on the ground, which is my mother's gate, I knock with my staff at all hours, and say, "Dear mother, let me in! Look how I am fading, flesh and blood and skin! Alas, when will my bones find a resting-place. Mother, I would exchange with you my chest of clothes which has been in my room for a long time, yes, for a hair-cloth shroud in which to wrap myself!" But she will not yet do me that favour, though my face is all pale and withered.

385 *An old man and a povre* . . .: The old man is a symbolic figure, representing goodness and humility. He stands in direct contrast to the revellers, who treat him rudely, thus epitomizing their contemptible and selfish way of life.

389 *carl*: Literally 'man', but used in a sneering sense.

394 *Inde*: India, indicating a far distance, the other side of the earth in medieval times.

399 *Ne deeth*: Note the effective contrast – the old man seeks death but cannot die, the revellers seek Death, and die.

401 *my modres gate*: The earth which bore the old man is his mother, the 'gate' is the way back to her. This is a vivid personification and has a moving, pathetic quality too.

406–8 *cheste . . . heyre clout*: The idea is to change the clothes worn in life with the simple shroud which covers the body in death.

But, sirs, to yow it is no curteisye
To speken to an old man vileinye,
But he trespasse in worde, or elles in dede.
In holy writ ye may your-self wel rede,
"Agayns an old man, hoor upon his heed,   415
Ye sholde aryse;" wherfor I yeve yow reed,
Ne dooth un-to an old man noon harm now,
Na-more than ye wolde men dide to yow
In age, if that ye so longe abyde;
And god be with yow, wher ye go or ryde.   420
I moot go thider as I have to go.'
    'Nay, olde cherl, by god, thou shalt nat so,'
Seyde this other hasardour anon;
'Thou partest nat so lightly, by seint Iohn!
Thou spak right now of thilke traitour Deeth,   425
That in this contree alle our frendes sleeth.
Have heer my trouthe, as thou art his aspye,
Tel wher he is, or thou shalt it abye,
By god, and by the holy sacrament!
For soothly thou art oon of his assent,   430
To sleen us yonge folk, thou false theef!'

'But, sirs, it is impolite of you to speak rudely to an old man unless he sins in word or deed. You may read for yourself in the Holy Writ "in the presence of an old white-haired man you should rise up (in respect)" – I commend this advice to you. Do not injure an old man now any more than you would wish man to do it to you when you are old, if you live that long. And God be with you wherever you walk or ride. I must go where I have to go.'

'No, old churl, by God you shall not do so,' quickly said one of the gamblers. 'You will not leave so easily, by St John. You spoke just now of that traitor Death who is killing all our friends in this country. On my honour, you are his spy! Tell us where he is, or you will pay for it, by God and by the Holy Sacrament. For truly you are in his conspiracy to murder us young people, you lying thief!'

415 '*Agayns an old man . . .*': See Leviticus 19:32, 'Thou shalt rise up before the hoary head, and honour the face of the old man.' He (like the Pardoner) is citing the Bible, here to stress the Christian code of respect for age which the revellers signally lack.

419 *if that ye so longe abyde*: This carries the implication perhaps that sinners may find death sooner than they expected – another ironic emphasis in view of the fate awaiting the revellers.

421 *thider as I have to go*: Not rambling, but a distinct destination, an acceptance of fate and, as he observed earlier, of the will of God.

424 *by seint Iohn*: Note the continuation of the blasphemy.

'Now, sirs,' quod he, 'if that yow be so leef
To finde Deeth, turne up this croked wey,
For in that grove I lafte him, by my fey,
Under a tree, and ther he wol abyde;   435
Nat for your boost he wol him no-thing hyde.
See ye that ook? right ther ye shul him finde.
God save yow, that boghte agayn mankinde,
And yow amende!' – thus seyde this olde man.
And everich of thise ryotoures ran,   440
Til he cam to that tree, and ther they founde
Of florins fyne of golde y-coyned rounde
Wel ny an eighte busshels, as hem thoughte.
No lenger thanne after Deeth they soughte,
But ech of hem so glad was of that sighte,   445
For that the florins been so faire and brighte,
That doun they sette hem by this precious hord.
The worste of hem he spake the firste word.

'Brethren,' quod he, 'tak kepe what I seye;
My wit is greet, though that I bourde and pleye.   450
This tresor hath fortune un-to us yiven,
In mirthe and Iolitee our lyf to liven,
And lightly as it comth, so wol we spende.
Ey! goddes precious dignitee! who wende
To-day, that we sholde han so fair a grace?   455

'Now gentlemen,' he (the old man) said, 'if you wish to find Death, follow this crooked path, for by my faith, I left him in that grove under a tree, and there he will wait. He will not hide because of your boast. Do you see that oak tree? Right there you will find him. May the God who redeemed mankind redeem you and improve you.' Thus said the old man, and each one of these revellers ran until he came to the tree. There they found, as they calculated, eight bushels of fine gold florin coins. They searched no longer for Death then, for each of them was so pleased with that sight – the florins being so attractive and bright – that they sat down by this precious hoard. The worst man among them was the first to speak.

'Brothers,' he said, 'take heed of what I say. My intelligence is good, although I joke and gamble. This treasure has been given to us by fortune so that we may live our lives in laughter and merriment, and we shall spend it as easily as it has come. Oh, God's precious nobleness! Who would have thought that we should have had such fine luck today?

433 *turne up this croked wey*: One of the key phrases in the tale. It is not just a direction, but the path that leads to sin, the money which the old man has left which provokes greed, treachery, murder. The revellers embrace moral death and meet with physical death.

442 *florins*: Each of these would be worth 33 pence in decimal currency, but represented wealth in Chaucer's time.

444 *No lenger thanne after Deeth they soughte*: Another ironic, almost casual statement – in effect they have found death, symbolized by the gold which is to kill them all.

453 *lightly as it comth*: Equivalent to the modern 'easy come, easy go', further pointing the moral of the tale.

But mighte this gold be caried fro this place
Hoom to myn hous, or elles un-to youres —
For wel ye woot that al this gold is oures —
Than were we in heigh felicitee.
But trewely, by daye it may nat be;   460
Men wolde seyn that we were theves stronge,
And for our owene tresor doon us honge,
This tresor moste y-caried be by nighte
As wysly and as slyly as it mighte.
Wherfore I rede that cut among us alle   465
Be drawe, and lat se wher the cut wol falle;
And he that hath the cut with herte blythe
Shal renne to the toune, and that ful swythe,
And bringe us breed and wyn ful prively.
And two of us shul kepen subtilly   470
This tresor wel; and, if he wol nat tarie,
Whan it is night, we wol this tresor carie
By oon assent, wher-as us thinketh best.'
That oon of hem the cut broughte in his fest,
And bad hem drawe, and loke wher it wol falle;   475
And it fil on the yongeste of hem alle;
And forth toward the toun he wente anon.
And al-so sone as that he was gon,
That oon of hem spak thus un-to that other,
'Thou knowest wel thou art my sworne brother,   480
Thy profit wol I telle thee anon.

But if this gold can be carried from here home to my house, or else to yours – for you well know that all this gold is ours – then we shall have great happiness. But certainly this cannot be done by day. Men would observe (or say) that we were strong thieves, and would hang us for having what is our own treasure. This treasure must be moved by night, as cleverly and as slyly as possible. Therefore I propose that we draw lots among us all, and let's see to whom the lot falls. And he who draws it will run quickly and uncomplainingly to the town, and will secretly fetch us bread and wine. And two of us will cunningly guard this treasure well; and if he doesn't delay, when it is night we will move this treasure by mutual agreement to where we think best.' Then one of them held the lots in his fist, and asked them to draw and see to whom it fell. And it fell on the youngest of them all, and he straightaway set out for the town. And just as soon as he was gone, one of them spoke in this way to the other, 'You know truly that you are my sworn brother, and I will now tell you something to your advantage.

459 *heigh felicitee*: The greatest happiness, but 'felicitee' implies 'blessedness' in the spiritual sense, the reverse of what the reveller means here.

465 *I rede that cut among us alle*: This refers to the drawing of lots, straws held in the hand, their length concealed. Here the youngest of the three revellers draws the shortest. Note that this action – dependent on chance – underpins the gambling motif.

469 *breed and wyn*: A subtle Chaucer reference to the Catholic Mass, where bread and wine symbolize the body and blood of Christ (see note l. 211). The Pardoner would be mindful of the effect this would have on his audience, particularly when said by the reveller who worships the Devil and not Christ.

480 *'Thou knowest wel . . .'*: Note the ease and naturalness of the dialogue, and also the narrative speed of the tale which keeps the audience at a pitch of excitement.

Thou woost wel that our felawe is agon;
And heer is gold, and that ful greet plentee,
That shal departed been among us three.
But natheles, if I can shape it so   485
That it departed were among us two,
Hadde I nat doon a freendes torn to thee?'
   That other answerde, 'I noot how that may be;
He woot how that the gold is with us tweye,
What shal we doon, what shal we to him seye?'   490
   'Shal it be conseil?' seyde the firste shrewe,
'And I shall tellen thee, in wordes fewe,
What we shal doon, and bringe it wel aboute.'
   'I graunte,' quod that other, 'out of doute,
That, by my trouthe, I wol thee nat biwreye.'   495
   'Now,' quod the firste, 'thou woost wel we be tweye,
And two of us shul strenger be than oon.
Look whan that he is set, and right anoon
Arys, as though thou woldest with him pleye;
And I shal ryve him thurgh the sydes tweye   500
Whyl that thou strogelest with him as in game,
And with thy dagger look thou do the same;
And than shal al this gold departed be,
My dere freend, bitwixen me and thee;
Than may we bothe our lustes al fulfille,   505
And pleye at dees right at our owene wille.'
And thus acorded been thise shrewes tweye
To sleen the thridde, as ye han herd me seye.

You are well aware that our comrade is gone, and that here is a great amount of gold which will be shared among the three of us. But nevertheless, if I can so contrive it that it is divided between the two of us, have I not done you a friendly turn?'

The other one answered, 'I don't see how that can be done. He knows for sure that the gold is here with us two. What shall we do? What shall we tell him?'

'Shall it be a secret?' said the first wretch, 'and shall I tell you in a few words what we shall do in order to accomplish it favourably?'

'I pledge without any doubt,' said the other, 'that on my word I will not betray you.'

'Now,' said the first, 'you can see clearly that we are two and that the two of us would be stronger than one. Make sure when he has sat down, and get up yourself immediately as though you were going to have fun with him. And I shall pierce him through both his sides while you wrestle with him as if in jest. And make sure that you do the same with your dagger. And then all this gold can be shared between you and me, my dear friend. Then we shall both fulfil all our desires and play at dice just as we please.' And thus these two wretches agreed to murder the third, as you have heard me describe.

495 *by my trouthe*: A meaningless oath which contrasts effectively with the blasphemous ones.
500 *I shal ryve him thurgh the sydes tweye*: This is a detail which maintains the association with Christ, an echo of the spear thrusts in Christ's side on the cross.

This yongest, which that wente un-to the toun,
Ful ofte in herte he rolleth up and doun   510
The beautee of thise florins newe and brighte.
'O lord!' quod he, 'if so were that I mighte
Have al this tresor to my-self allone,
Ther is no man that liveth under the trone
Of god, that sholde live so mery as I!'   515
And atte laste the feend, our enemy,
Putte in his thought that he shold poyson beye,
With which he mighte sleen his felawes tweye;
For-why the feend fond him in swich lyvinge,
That he had leve him to sorwe bringe,   520
For this was outrely his fulle entente
To sleen hem bothe, and never to repente.
And forth he gooth, no lenger wolde he tarie,
Into the toun, un-to a pothecarie,
And preyed him, that he him wolde selle   525
Som poyson, that he mighte his rattes quelle;
And eek ther was a polcat in his hawe,
That, as he seyde, his capouns hadde y-slawe,
And fayn he wolde wreke him, if he mighte,
On vermin, that destroyed him by nighte.   530

The youngest, who went into the town, continually turned over in his mind the beauty of those bright new florins. 'O Lord,' he said, 'if it were possible that I might have all this treasure completely to myself, there is no man living under the throne of God who would live as merrily as I!' And at last the Devil our enemy put into his mind the idea that he should buy poison with which to kill his two companions. For since the Devil found him living in such a manner he had the right to bring him to sorrow. For his full and considered intention was to kill them both and never to repent of it. And off he went – no longer would he delay – into the town, to a chemist, and asked him if he would sell him some poison so that he could destroy his rats. And also there was a polecat in his yard, which, he said, had killed his chickens. And he would like to exact revenge, if he could, on vermin which were injuring him by night.

526–7 *his rattes ... a polcat*: 'rattes' suggests by association his 'friends', the vermin of society because of their sins. The polecat is a small creature like a weasel which gives off an offensive smell. They were reasonably common in Chaucer's time.

530 *On vermin*: A distinct reference to his companions, who have, unbeknown to him, already made their plans to destroy him.

The pothecarie answerde, 'and thou shalt have
A thing that, al-so god my soule save,
In al this world ther nis no creature,
That ete or dronke hath of this confiture
Noght but the mountance of a corn of whete, 535
That he ne shal his lyf anon forlete;
Ye, sterve he shal, and that in lasse whyle
Than thou wolt goon a paas nat but a myle;
This poyson is so strong and violent.'
  This cursed man hath in his hond y-hent 540
This poyson in a box, and sith he ran
In-to the nexte strete, un-to a man,
And borwed [of] him large botels three;
And in the two his poyson poured he;
The thridde he kepte clene for his drinke. 545
For al the night he shoop him for to swinke
In caryinge of the gold out of that place.
And whan this ryotour, with sory grace,
Had filled with wyn his grete botels three,
To his felawes agayn repaireth he. 550
What nedeth it to sermone of it more?
For right as they had cast his deeth bifore,
Right so they han him slayn, and that anon.
And whan that this was doon, thus spak that oon,
'Now lat us sitte and drinke, and make us merie, 555
And afterward we wol his body berie.'

The chemist answered, 'And you shall have something, God protect my soul, which will kill any creature in the world after it has eaten and drunk of this preparation, even an amount which is only the size of a grain of corn. Yes, it will die, and that in a shorter time than you would walk a mile at a steady pace, this poison is so strong and violent (in its effects).'

This cursed man seized the box of poison in his hand, and then he ran into the next street to a man from whom he borrowed three large bottles. He poured the poison into two of these, and kept the third clean for his own drink. For he planned to toil throughout the night in removing the gold from that place. And when this reveller – bad luck to him! – had filled his three large bottles with wine, he returned to his companions.

What need is there to preach any more about it? For just as they had planned his death beforehand, so they proceeded at once to kill him. And when this was done, one of them said, 'Now let us sit down, drink, and be merry, and afterwards, we will bury his body.'

540 *This cursed man . . .*: This and the following lines maintain the speed of the narrative, which reflects the quickness of the reveller's mind and actions in his determination to kill and thus have all for himself – an exact duplication of his companions' plans, too.

551 *What nedeth it to sermone . . .*: Note the sudden end to the narrative, a masterly way of defining the inevitable end of wickedness, the finality of death. The three revellers are killed off in nine lines, destroyed by their own evil. The moral has been adroitly demonstrated.

And with that word it happed him, par cas,
To take the botel ther the poyson was,
And drank, and yaf his felawe drinke also,
For which anon they storven bothe two.   560
  But, certes, I suppose that Avicen
Wroot never in no canon, ne in no fen,
Mo wonder signes of empoisoning
Than hadde thise wrecches two, er hir ending.
Thus ended been thise homicydes two,   565
And eek the false empoysoner also.

  O cursed sinne, ful of cursednesse!
O traytours homicyde, o wikkednesse!
O glotonye, luxurie, and hasardrye!
Thou blasphemour of Crist with vileinye   570
And othes grete, of usage and of pryde!
Allas! mankinde, how may it bityde,
That to thy creatour which that thee wroghte,
And with his precious herte-blood thee boghte,
Thou art so fals and so unkinde, allas!   575

And with these words it happened to him by chance to pick up the bottle containing the poison, and drink, and give it to his companion to drink as well, as a result of which they both died.

But assuredly I believe that Avicenna never wrote in any rule or section about more wondrous signs of poisoning than these two wretches showed before they died. Thus these two murderers met their deaths as well as the lying poisoner.

O accursed sin, full of wickeness! O treacherous murder, O damnable behaviour, O gluttony, lust and gambling! You blasphemer of Christ through your wickedness and great oaths (uttered) from habit and pride. Alas, mankind, how did it come to pass, that to the creator who made you and redeemed you with his precious heart's blood, you are so treacherous and unnatural?

560 *For which anon they storven . . .*: The two deaths in one line is a deliberate anti-climax, almost as if sinners are beyond further consideration.

561 *Avicen*: This is Ibn Sina, Avicenna (980–1037), the Arab medical authority whose famous treatise on medicine was divided into sections (fens) and defined manner of proceeding (canon).

562 *Wroot never in no canon*: See the preceding note. Apart from displaying his wide learning again, the Pardoner is anxious to impress upon his audience that the revellers died horrible deaths for their sins.

Now, goode men, god forgeve yow your trespas,
And ware yow fro the sinne of avaryce.
Myn holy pardoun may yow alle waryce,
So that ye offre nobles or sterlinges,
Or elles silver broches, spones, ringes.   580
Boweth your heed under this holy bulle!
Cometh up, ye wyves, offreth of your wolle!
Your name I entre heer in my rolle anon;
In-to the blisse of hevene shul ye gon;
I yow assoile, by myn heigh power,   585
Yow that wol offre, as clene and eek as cleer
As ye were born; and, lo, sirs, thus I preche.
And Iesu Crist, that is our soules leche,
So graunte yow his pardon to receyve;
For that is best; I wol yow nat deceyve.   590

Now good men, may God forgive you your trespasses and warn you from the sin of avarice. My holy pardon may heal you all, so offer gold or silver coins, or else silver brooches, spoons or rings. Bow your head beneath this holy bull! Come forward, you wives, make offerings of your wool! I will then enter your names in my roll here, and you will proceed to the bliss of heaven. I absolve you by my great authority – those (that is) who make offerings – as pure and innocent as when you were born. And look, good people, this is how I preach. And Jesus Christ, who is the healer of our souls, grants you to receive his pardon, for that is the best way, I will not deceive you.

577 *the sinne of avaryce*: The Pardoner has illustrated his theme through authority and the tale, but naturally it doesn't stop him practising what he preaches against.

579 *nobles or sterlinges*: The value of the first would be about 33 pence in decimal currency (though worth much more in Chaucer's day). Sterlinges are silver pennies, sterling coins.

580 *silver broches, spones, ringes*: These are an indication of the Pardoner's 'avaryce'. Goods in kind were acceptable to him, thus underlining his commercial rather than his spiritual concerns – they might prove to be more valuable than money!

583 *Your name I entre*: The Pardoner sets the seal on his spurious authority by making a list of those who, because of their 'offerings', will find the way to heaven. The pilgrims, however, do not constitute the usual credulous audience!

585 *I yow assoile*: This is effectively the end of the sermon. The Pardoner makes the high but false claim that he has the power of absolution, something reserved for priests and, ultimately, God.

But sirs, o word forgat I in my tale,
I have relikes and pardon in my male,
As faire as any man in Engelond,
Whiche were me yeven by the popes hond.
If any of yow wol, of devocioun,   595
Offren, and han myn absolucioun,
Cometh forth anon, and kneleth heer adoun,
And mekely receyveth my pardoun:
Or elles, taketh pardon as ye wende,
Al newe and fresh, at every tounes ende,   600
So that ye offren alwey newe and newe
Nobles and pens, which that be gode and trewe.
It is an honour to everich that is heer,
That ye mowe have a suffisant pardoneer
Tassoille yow, in contree as ye ryde,   605
For aventures which that may bityde.
Peraventure ther may falle oon or two
Doun of his hors, and breke his nekke atwo.
Look which a seuretee is it to yow alle
That I am in your felaweship y-falle,   610
That may assoille yow, bothe more and lasse,
Whan that the soule shal fro the body passe.
I rede that our hoste heer shal biginne,
For he is most envoluped in sinne.
Com forth, sir hoste, and offre first anon,   615
And thou shalt kisse the reliks everichon,
Ye, for a grote! unbokel anon thy purs.'

But good people, I forgot one thing in my story. I have relics and pardons in my bag as fine as anyone in England, which I received from the Pope's hands. If any of you, out of devoutness, make an offering and receive my absolution, come forth straightaway and kneel down here, and humbly receive my pardon. Alternatively, be freshly pardoned as you are going along, at the limits of every town, provided that you always offer again and again gold coins or pennies which are sound and genuine. It is an honour for everyone here that you have a competent pardoner to absolve you as you ride through the countryside, regardless of any adventures which may befall you. By mischance one or two may fall from his horse and break his neck in two. Look what a reassurance it is to you all that I have joined you, so that I can absolve you, both the noble and the low-born when the time comes for the soul to pass from the body. I advise that our Host should begin, for he is the most involved in sinful ways. Come forth, sir Host, and then make your first offering, and you shall kiss each of my relics, yes, for a groat. Then undo your purse.'

591 *But sirs, o word forgat I in my tale*: This signals the return to his own sales-talk, somewhat brazen, since he is asking the pilgrims to 'offer' though he has already boasted of his own capacity to swindle. He is, as ever, seizing the opportunity for quick profit, even throwing in the transparent lie that his relics were given to him by the Pope.

604 *a suffisant pardoneer*: He is setting himself up as a spiritual doctor; he is of course a quack.

608 *and breke his nekke atwo*: The Pardoner appears to have gone too far. There is a kind of spite in this which, doubtless, contributes to the anger of the Host when he is addressed.

613 *out hoste heer*: The Pardoner has misjudged his man. Harry Bailly answers this with an attack of concentrated obscenity. He obviously despises the Pardoner and sees right through him.

'Nay, nay,' quod he, 'than have I Cristes curs!
Lat be,' quod he, 'it shal nat be, so theech!
Thou woldest make me kisse thyn old breech,   620
And swere it were a relik of a seint,
Thogh it were with thy fundement depeint!
But by the croys which that seint Eleyne fond,
I wolde I hadde thy coillons in myn hond
In stede of relikes or of seintuarie;   625
Lat cutte hem of, I wol thee helpe hem carie;
Thay shul be shryned in an hogges tord.'
   This pardoner answerde nat a word;
So wrooth he was, no word ne wolde he seye.
   'Now,' quod our host, 'I wol no lenger pleye   630
With thee, ne with noon other angry man.'
But right anon the worthy knight bigan,
Whan that he saugh that al the peple lough,
'Na-more of this, for it is right y-nough;
Sir pardoner, be glad and mery of chere;   635
And ye, sir host, that been to me so dere,
I prey yow that ye kisse the pardoner.
And pardoner, I prey thee, drawe thee neer,
And, as we diden, lat us laughe and pleye.'
Anon they kiste, and riden forth hir weye.   640

Here is ended the Pardoners Tale.

'No, no,' he (the Host) cried, 'then I would have Christ's curse! Give up,' he said, 'it shall not be, so may I prosper. You would make me kiss your old breeches and swear that it was the relic of a saint though it was stained from your arse. But by the cross which St Helena found, I wish I had your testicles in my hand instead of relics or a sacred box. Let them be cut off – I will help you carry them – they shall be enshrined in a pig's shit.'

To this the Pardoner made no reply; he was so angry that he would not say a word.

'Now,' said our Host, 'I will no longer joke with you or with any other angry man.' But right then the good Knight interrupted when he saw that all the people were laughing, 'No more of this, for that is enough! Sir Pardoner, be glad and of good heart, and you, Sir Host, who have been so dear to me, I ask you to kiss the Pardoner. And Pardoner, I ask you to come nearer and, as we were doing, let us laugh and joke.' Then they kissed, and they rode off on their way.

623 *seint Eleyne*: St Helena (A.D. ?255–330) was the mother of the Emperor Constantine the Great (A.D. ?280–337) who was the first Christian Roman ruler. She was believed to have found the real cross on which Christ was crucified. The Host is thus swearing on what he believes to be a true relic as distinct from the Pardoner's fake ones.

632 *the worthy knight*: It is fitting that the Knight, highest in social status among the pilgrims, and morally pre-eminent too, should act as peacemaker in this quarrel. Not only does this smooth the pilgrimage and pave the way for the next Tale, it is also a genuine Christian action following on the spurious Christian attitude of the Pardoner.

Structural Summary

This should be read in conjunction with the text itself, and the student should glance across at the critical commentary on 'The Pardoner's Character' and the relevant sections of 'Chaucer's Art'.

THE WORDS OF THE HOST

Before the Pardoner's Prologue, the Host responds to *The Physician's Tale* which has just been concluded. It shows again Chaucer's overall awareness of structure that the tale told by the curer and healer of the flesh should be followed by a tale told by the spurious curer and healer of souls. But this is typical Chaucerian irony. Though the Host is a coarse but likeable man, he is also intensely subjective and emotional, easily moved to tears or anger, a volatile character. The Physician has just told the tale of the beautiful girl Virginia who attracts the attention of a judge. This corrupt man determines that he will possess her sexually and concocts a plot to steal her from her father on the evidence of a treacherous ally. The father realizes that she is destined for a life of dishonour and kills her rather than make her over to the judge. In the ensuing popular outcry on behalf of the father, the judge is gaoled himself and commits suicide. The Host is greatly moved and moralizes as follows:

> That yiftes of fortune or of nature
> Ben cause of deeth to many a creature.
> Hir beautee was hir deeth, I dar wel sayn;
> Allas! so pitously as she was slayn!

After expressing some pride in the repetition of these sentiments, the Host takes delight (his volatility is in evidence) in mocking the Physician by using some technical medical terms like 'urinals' (jars for holding urine) and 'Galianes', which were probably drinks, their name being derived from the medical authority of ancient times, Galen (A.D. ?130–?200). He now wants a tale to cheer him up and, with tongue in cheek we suspect, turns to his 'bel amy' the Pardoner and asks him to 'Tel us som mirthe or Iapes right anon.' The Pardoner, possibly fooled or flattered, agrees to do so after he has had something to drink and eat, but the more genteel pilgrims object to this (it shows how the Pardoner is despised by his social betters), thinking that he will offer a salacious story, and they demand a Tale which is morally uplifting. The Pardoner responds with a vengeance, but affects to be thinking of the right moral Tale while he is having a drink.

THE PARDONER'S PROLOGUE

(Lines 1–6)   The Prologue falls into a number of divisions which show how cunningly the Pardoner works on the minds of his usual audience. They also expose him for the villain he is. Remember that he is confiding in the audience of pilgrims, confessing at the same time, and elaborating and detailing his methods as he goes. He always sticks to a common theme (the love of money is the root of all evil) and he knows what he preaches by heart.

(Lines 7–48)   The section which follows the introduction deals with the evidences of his authority, both genuine and false and, after the preliminary of a few impressive words in Latin, he displays his relics. These he relates directly to the needs of his usual audience, playing on their superstition by suggesting that these relics can provide cures, even a cure for jealousy, or an increase in crops, always provided that suitable offerings are made to him, the Pardoner, for these relics.

(Lines 49–60)   The next section finds the Pardoner again playing on his audience. No one who 'doon sinne horrible' can make any offers to his relics, though any one of the lesser sinners may do so. The Pardoner is an experienced student of human nature, and knows that no one will admit outwardly that he/she has committed adultery, for example, and therefore all his usual congregation are eligible to bid for the relics.

(Lines 61–94)   The Pardoner now turns to his present audience of pilgrims. He boasts of his income from this trick, and brags about the quality of the deception he practises in his preaching. He takes a great delight in the figure he presents to his (usual) audience, and his emphasis is self-congratulatory. He knows how good he is and is determined to impress the pilgrims with a consciousness of his manner. He then confesses that he only preaches for profit, that he doesn't care if those he absolves are damned, and asserts that many a good sermon is preached from evil intentions. He asserts that he is quite capable of publicly exposing those who have dared to be critical of pardoners, not naming them by name, but making sure that the audience know who they are. And, says the Pardoner, he himself does this under the guise of holiness.

(Lines 95–106)   The Pardoner next argues that his theme is

particularly suited to him for although he is a greedy man himself yet he can successfuly preach against avarice; it is his individual quality to be able to turn his audience towards repentance. He further re-iterates that he himself only preaches for profit. The Prologue and the Tale depend partly for their effect on repetition, a quality which most public speakers employ, particularly if their audience is unsophisticated and has no copy of what is being said, as here.

(Lines 107–134)   The Pardoner refers to his basic technique of illustrating his theme from the 'olde stories' (or *exempla*) since these are readily retained by simple folk. He then turns to his present audience and tells them that he will not dream of being poor and undertaking manual labour while he has the opportunity to gain rich rewards through his preaching. He describes all the good things in life that he can have and then, having had the drink he wanted, he says that he, 'a ful vicious man/A moral tale yet I yow telle can'. Note that we have come back to the starting point – the request from the refined pilgrims for just such a tale. We should also note that the tipsy Pardoner has condemned himself out of his own mouth. We know he is a fraud.

THE PARDONER'S TALE

(Lines 135–156)   The Pardoner appears to be plunging straight into his story judging from the first twenty lines, which take us almost up to the end of the initial paragraph. But this is not so. The appetite is whetted by the beginning of the Tale, but into that beginning the Pardoner lists the main sins that he is going to attack. Gluttony, gambling, and particularly swearing figure prominently, but the Pardoner is determined to break off the tale. This is a tantalizing manoeuvre, since the narrative in those first twenty lines is already flowing in a vivid and sensual way. However, the Pardoner's plan involves the citing of examples and comments on the nature of sin. There is therefore a mention of 'holy writ' at the end of his verse paragraph.

(Lines 157–176)   The first assault is on drunkenness and the examples have a cumulative effect. Three lines are devoted to Lot, four to Herod and John the Baptist and then, a typical departure, a movement away from the Bible, here to Seneca, with six lines allocated to his equation of madness and drunkenness. It will be seen from this that there is a deliberate rhetorical build up (bombastic, concentrating on effect), preparing the way for the apostrophizing (here, personification) of gluttony which occurs immediately after the example of Seneca. The repeated 'O's' show the Pardoner bewailing *and* cursing, achieving a kind of crescendo before proceeding to his next example.

(Lines 177–200) By now in full flow, the Pardoner maintains that Adam's sin was gluttony, which is absurd since Adam did not eat the apple simply because he was hungry. The seven lines given to this precede another apostrophizing of gluttony. The warning to man to be careful of his diet is put in the kind of sensual language which itself constitutes temptation ('the shorte throte, the tendre mouth') and it leads to another biblical strengthening, this time with reference to St Paul. The final few lines of the paragraph are notable for the return to the effects of drink and the strong language in which the condemnation is couched – 'That of his throte he maketh his privee'.

(Lines 201–220) The last image is virtually continued in the next paragraph after another instance from St Paul, with phrases like 'stinking cod', 'Fulfild of donge' and 'foul is the soun'. Notice that drinking and gluttony are associated throughout, and that the alternations of the speaker's mood are calculated to play on the emotions (and the guilt) of his usual audience. Thus in the course of four lines here the Pardoner is able to move from 'I seye it now weping with pitous voys' to 'O wombe! O bely! O stinking cod'. One of the major techniques used by the Pardoner is this change of mood – from pathos, to frenzied denunciation, to the next example. He also here dwells on the preparation of food, almost suggesting that cooks themselves corrupt food in their searches for the many concoctions which delight the glutton. Again these descriptions are followed by the defining of the sin, here compared to death. This picking up of the main substance of the coming story is evidence of the structural cohesion which is apparent throughout the Pardoner's address and through all his transitions of mood.

(Lines 221–244) *The Pardoner's Tale*, as I have indicated, is often markedly physical in its stress. The reversion to drunkenness now takes the form of the revolting appearance and noises of the drunken man, the 'Sampsoun' sound, as I have said elsewhere in this commentary (p. 63), being an inspired and ironical example. The Pardoner dwells on these details with a kind of sadistic pleasure in order to spell out physical deterioration and degradation. We note particularly two lines which have a direct bearing on the cautionary tale to come:

> In whom that drinke hath dominacioun,
> He can no conseil kepe, it is no drede.

It is certain that when the revellers set out in search of Death that they are drunk, and they cannot prevent the secret they have discovered (the treasure) from corrupting them and being responsible for their deaths. The second part of this denunciation is given over to a contemporary reference which would not be lost on either of his audiences. The commercial malpractice of mixing cheap and expensive wines, and doubtless passing them off as being of superior quality, is a form of corruption which complements both the corruption of the body through excess, *and* the corruption of the Pardoner, who is himself guilty of excessive deception. The theme of corruption in *The Pardoner's Tale* always carries this duality of interpretation, and here the repetition of the word 'Sampsoun' at the end of the section provides the physical stamp of degradation which is the lot of the drunkard.

(Lines 245–260) The final section on drunkenness follows the established pattern of this particular sermon, and note that the sermon is appropriate to both audiences, the present one of pilgrims and the common audiences who are played and preyed upon by the Pardoner. The Pardoner advocates abstinence and prayer, as usual referring to the Bible, here interestingly to the Old Testament, and then mixes his references, the first to the all-conquering Attila, and then to Lemuel. Pagan and biblical authorities can both be made to subserve his purpose. He is also preparing the way for other examples of men in high places being guilty of the sin of gambling in the next section. Having made his point through examples and reiteration, he brings the theme of gluttony to a close and turns to the next of the major sins with which he is dealing: gambling.

(Lines 261–300) The indiscriminate listing of the various vices which opens the section on gambling has been referred to elsewhere in this commentary. The introduction prepares us for the approach through the examples to come of princes and rulers who abuse their position through this vice. In preaching to the low and the mixed he naturally chooses the high by way of illustration. The example of 'Stilbon' seems rather verbose, until we consider that it exactly fits one of the Pardoner's assertions, namely that gambling wastes time. By demonstrating that the ambassador has undertaken a long journey only to find 'alle the grettest that were of that lond' gambling is in itself a waste of time. This is evidence of the tightness of construction, the running relevance mentioned earlier. Of course it also makes the point that men of honour reject the vice of gambling. The use of direct speech in the character of the ambassador is very effective. The Pardoner is not merely quoting, he is projecting himself into the character part, cunningly associating himself with such a man of honour. The example of King Demetrius again closes with the kind of statement which perhaps unwittingly reveals the Pardoner's cynicism. He observes

> Lordes may finden other maner pley
> Honeste y-nough to dryve the day awey.

I suggest that this is said tongue-in-cheek, with a deliberately sarcastic use of the word 'honeste'. What the Pardoner is really saying is that anything else done by rulers is not relevant to his argument, therefore it does not matter what they do. This section on gambling is beautifully balanced between the statement, the long first example and the concluding second example. The plan of the sermon is becoming more apparent.

(Lines 301–332) The final section on swearing completes the long and sometimes tantalizing delay before the actual Tale. The psychological effect of the Pardoner's method is (a) to enable him to get at his audience both directly and by using analogy or stories and (b) to arouse excitement by delaying the tale until his audience has been fully educated for it. The attack on swearing would have immediate and direct impact, for many of his audience – Harry Bailly in particular – would swear either casually or seriously or both. This is probably why the Pardoner makes it the climax of his address, since it is calculated to invoke feelings of guilt – and with the staring eyes of the speaker none would feel safe from his scrutiny. The distinction is made between 'Gret swering' and 'false swering' and the authorities cited here are all biblical, with the Ten Commandments having pride of place, though the Pardoner's evaluation of the relative importance of them is certainly an individual one. Again one suspects that the reason for this is that it suits his emphasis, and also that by climaxing his statements with the Commandments he is actually using – very effective dramatically – the voice of God. The plan of this section, like those of the others, is to finish on a high note; put briefly, all the authorities cited are impressive but the most impressive of all is God himself. The actual quoting of oaths anticipates the many oaths used in the Tale itself, and a cunning reference to oaths used in gambling is worked in – 'the bicched bones two'.

THE TALE

(Lines 333–363)   The picking up of the Tale is adroitly managed. The revellers are drinking although it is so early in the day – perhaps it is implied that they have been drinking all night. In an earlier statement the Pardoner has said that anyone practising gluttony or drunkenness is already dead, and these three find death already close to them in the form of the corpse about to be buried. Structurally, this is a clever use of association, death being both moral and physical, and the fact that the boy tells them that the dead man was 'an old felawe of youres' reinforces the association. Although Death is symbolized in the boy's account, the fact is that the man died while he was drunk, thus confirming the Pardoner's example of Attila. We note the boy's warning to the revellers. He is repeating what his mother has told him, but between the lines is the comment that if you live an evil life you die – therefore turn away from the evil life. In going straight out to search for Death the revellers are following the evil life, a life which they will not forsake. There is also a fine equation of the pestilence with death and the emphatic atmosphere of death surrounding all. Yet the reality – the tavern, the dead man, the boy's account, the publican's reference to the 'greet village' – is evocative of medieval life, making the audience almost part of the story because of their identification with the setting and the events.

(Lines 364–382)   This marks the response of the rioters and the simple acceptance of the symbol of death as a reality which they can kill. Here the folk-tale element predominates – the Pardoner is aware of his simple audience as well as the more sophisticated one which is now listening to him, so that another of the virtues of the Tale itself is that it can be taken in a literal or symbolic way. The first reveller's speech is punctuated with oaths and, as we have seen, the false oath of blood brotherhood as well, which is so quickly to be abused. There is a neat balance struck between the speed of idea, the swearing to be brothers and the determination to kill Death on the one hand, and the description of their setting out for the village having taken their oaths and uttering many more blasphemies. I say a neat balance, because the direct speech indicates decision and forthcoming action, whereas the description of what they do allows the Pardoner to comment in his own voice on their blasphemy and the important fact that they are drunk.

(Lines 383–410)   The function of the old man and the role he plays have been examined elsewhere in this study on p. 77. The balance struck in the first eight lines is that between humility and disrespect, goodness and courtesy as against abuse and insensitivity. It doesn't really matter whether the old man symbolizes simply old age close to death, or the Wandering Jew who has no home and is compelled to wander ceaselessly about the world. The fact is that in selecting him through the Pardoner, Chaucer has shown an acute structural awareness. The old man is seeking Death which the revellers have already found – at least in the moral sense – yet, although the old man cannot find actual Death itself he can direct the revellers to him. Once more we note the balance. Moreover, the old man becomes a character in the Tale, pathetic, gentle, seeking, but unlike the revellers, not finding death. He represents the effects of the inevitable passage of time, and in the moral structure of the Tale is important too. No one that he meets will exchange his youth for the old man's age, a clear underlining of the fact that (a) nothing can be changed, for the passage of time marks us all and we can never turn time back, and (b) that whatever we do, we cannot change, there is no going back. I suggest that this is yet another comment within the Tale by Chaucer on the Pardoner's practice, that sins committed in the past cannot be wiped out by present repentance before someone not qualified to grant absolution. If you like, all life, sins and time can only be judged by God.

(Lines 411–421) Reference has been made to the fact that the old man cites the holy writ like the Pardoner, a very interesting device in view of the obviously intended difference in character of the two. It is also interesting that the old man seems to cast doubt on whether the revellers will live to be old (almost as if he has a prophetic insight), gives them God's blessing (straightforwardly or ironically?) and continues on his way in acceptance of his fate.

(Lines 422–448) The reveller commands the old man to tell him where Death is, and continues with his swearing. The oaths of course contrast with the blessing of the old man. The latter's reply is brief and to the point; they will find Death by the oak tree, and again the old man concludes with a blessing. The rioters quickly find the gold. The structure here is of question, reply, description, all of which hasten the narrative on until the worst of the revellers reveals his plan. This is a sharp sequence imbued with the directness we have come to expect within the Tale itself.

(Lines 449–477) The essential thing now is for the treasure to be moved by night so that no one will see the revellers. The drawing of lots would again be a commonplace contemporary way of coming to decisions, and there is a certain truth in the idea that 'My wit is greet, though that I bourde and pleye', for gambling does breed a kind of cunning in the attempt to outwit your opponent. Everything is now done at speed: the plan is made quickly, the drawing of lots is soon undertaken, the youngest departs for the town, the section is effectively over. The next two sections act as counterbalance to each other.

(Lines 478–508) This section contains the plan of one of the revellers to his 'sworne brother' to kill the third reveller who has gone to the town to get the bread and wine. The ensuing dialogue in which the second reveller does not immediately understand what his companion is driving at, followed by that companion's full explanation of the plan, is wonderfully economical. Just as no opportunity is wasted in order to get the treasure, so no words are wasted in describing the manner in which these two villains intend to obtain it. Throughout the structure run the moral comments, and there it seems that the motive for gaining the treasure is so that they may continue in their present way of life, more self-indulgently and wickedly than ever:

> Than may we bothe our lustes al fulfille,
> And pleye at dees right at our owene wille

(Lines 509–530) The first plan is spoken outwardly, the audience knowing what it is from the actual words. This is complemented by the inward temptation of the youngest reveller as he goes towards the town moved by the contemplation of the treasure and seduced by 'the feend, our enemy', who was able to corrupt him further because he was already living a corrupt life. The Pardoner therefore narrates his plan, the purchase of the poison. Corruption breeds corruption, and both these sections illustrate that a sworn oath between criminals is meaningless and can be broken with the coming of an idea. Treachery rules; the youngest buys poison to kill the 'vermin' which trouble him, while those moral vermin, his companions, have already plotted his own death.

(Lines 531–560) The speed which has characterized the narrative is now brought to a climax as the chemist boasts of the effectiveness of the poison, the youngest reveller hurriedly buys it and gets three bottles, into two of which he puts poison. He returns to his companions and here, beginning a new paragraph, the Pardoner, who has more than made his point through the story, breaks off to ask what is the point of continuing. It is a brief aside, however, to remind the audience that it is a story. He returns to it for the final flurry of death. All the revellers find what they have been searching for. That is the final irony of the story.

(Lines 561–575) The Pardoner turns to his final authority, here a medieval medical one, further playing on his audience's feelings by taking a sadistic pleasure in the agonies endured by the two revellers who inadvertently took the poison. It is a brief reference, but it re-establishes the method of the sermon now that the Tale itself is finished. Fearful of anti-climax, the Pardoner quickly adopts his usual apostrophizing rhetoric in which the sins he has dwelt on – and others – are forcefully condemned yet again. He asks, in another transition, how it is that mankind can be so cruel to the Saviour. Despite the speed of movement, the pattern is the same; example, rhetoric, pathos or a variation in order of these. The Pardoner is still sticking to his script.

(Lines 576–617) The sermon being ended, the Pardoner resumes his patter. He claims the power to grant absolution, asks his audience to come up with their gifts of money and of goods, and expresses the wish that Christ may bless them and pardon them, he will not deceive them on that matter. Having uttered this moving admission, he then contradicts it in spirit by proceeding to recommend his relics and pardons, claiming to have obtained them from the Pope. The alternative for those not yet receiving absolution at the moment is to receive it on the journey, the Pardoner even appearing to enjoy the fact that one or two of them may suffer accidents where they will be in need of 'a suffisant pardoneer/Tassoille yow'. This naturally sets him off boasting again, he becomes over-confident and even perhaps sure of the audience before him, tells the Host that he is 'most envoluped in sinne' and invites him to kiss the relics for the payment merely of a groat. The Pardoner cannot forget his own image. He has to act, motivated by greed rather than by reason, though in view of the remarks made by the Host earlier the Pardoner's invitation to him may have something of malice in it.

(Lines 618–640) The conclusion of the Tale shows the unequivocal and coarse response of the Host to the Pardoner's invitation, which is regarded as an insult. Although the language is obscene, it reduces the Pardoner to silent anger, for it is the language of exposure destructive of his image. It is the ridicule which hurts deeply. The Pardoner takes his function seriously and believes in it. But structurally the Host's words are very important. The audience and we as listeners have been treated to a performance which is in itself a form of blasphemy, and the Host's reaction is a spirited rejection of what is false. The extreme language is suitable to this easily-moved man, and once the Pardoner's spell is broken our own distaste and contempt are reasserted. Fake Christian practice is followed by genuine (in motive) Christian reconciliation. The action of the Knight is expressive of a broad tolerance, a tolerance obviously shared by the author, who has shown us the magnetic abilities of an unattractive and unscrupulous man, a spellbinder, a charlatan, an opportunist but one who is not beyond the bounds of Christian influence for all his abuse of it.

The Pardoner's Character

The Pardoner is described in selective detail in the general *Prologue to the Canterbury Tales* and these details provide important clues to the character of the man as it is revealed in his Tale. First, he obviously thinks of himself as someone of importance, riding in the latest manner, wearing his hair in a fashionable way, singing with the Summoner a rather worldly song despite their religious affiliations. He has 'staring' eyes, perhaps indicative of the excitable quality which he is able to introduce so easily into his Tale as he sets to work on the emotions and sense of guilt in his audience. He is ostentatious, a shameless commercial traveller dealing in spiritual goods, his St Veronica's badge a kind of advertisement, his wallet chock-full of pardons. Yet there is something ludicrous, even grotesque about him, for he has a voice as feeble as a goat's, is smooth-cheeked, a eunuch, and yet we are told that he could read a lesson in church superbly and that best of all was his rendering of the offertory. This would appear to contradict his having a goat-like voice; though the reference here is to his singing, there is little doubt that his preaching voice takes on greater power.

The Pardoner is the last of the pilgrims to be described, and this reflects perhaps Chaucer's own valuation of him in terms of his debased status, the moral comment on a corrupt profession and its representative. He and the Summoner are brothers in corruption, and thus the Pardoner's choice of this companion (or perhaps they chose each other) is a moral index to his character. Chaucer's mention of Rouncival and Rome are further indications of the Pardoner's malpractices, the first because it was connected with scandals over the collection of money, the second because the Pardoner's claim to have come from Rome, with its implication of Papal authority for his particular mission, was false, like so many others of his time.

The physical appearance of the Pardoner is unattractive and he is presented as sexually neuter. If the physical appearance reflects character, as the medieval mind believed, then the Pardoner's spiritual and moral deficiencies are in direct relation to that appearance. Yet it would be wrong to see the Pardoner only in this light. Chaucer subtly, and in very few words, arouses speculation about him in the reader, but he also redresses the balance, though of course with familiar irony. Quite simply, the Pardoner is good at his job, and I use the word 'job' because it is sufficiently removed from any spiritual context. In the Prologue Chaucer emphasizes his efficiency, for there is no other spiritual con-man to match him. The fact that he has brought so many relics, each with its prepared history, shows his ability to organize his material and present it with obvious relish. There is little doubt that he is an ingenious maker of stories which would have an authentic ring to a credulous audience. Having said this, Chaucer stresses his unscrupulousness and his trickery, the fact that he makes great profit while the poor Parson has to be content with mere existence. In some ways the Pardoner is used as part of Chaucer's attack on corruption in the Church, for only the Parson among the clerical characters in the General Prologue is described favourably. He is not a 'mercenarie'; by implication, the other ecclesiastical figures are, none more so than the Pardoner and his hideously-spotted (physically and spiritually) friend the Summoner.

In his own Prologue the Pardoner displays his techniques as well as his authorities and relics. His is the kind of salesmanship which relies on verbal and physical demonstration, and he is adept at both. In modern terms, he has a sound knowledge of psychology, knowing that nothing impresses like supposed evidence, that the simple mind responds to what it thinks it sees, and that it lacks the knowledge or the sophistication to question what it hears. There is something at once boastful and, strangely, honest about his account of his approach to his audiences. He always takes the same text, and he is a slave to that text in life, for money is the root of his particular evil. It is his motivation, his usage and abusage of the Church. He has a set technique, knowing that a few words of Latin will establish his authenticity. That done, he plays on the superstitious nature of his audience, again sound psychology, for there is an element of superstition in all of us. With farming, small-holding and poor rustic communities as the staple content of his audiences, he is able to fabricate the miraculous cure (cunningly in the tradition of some of the Christian miracles) whereby diseased cattle will not only be cured but will multiply, crops will increase, in short, life will become better for those who know hardship.

This is spurious and dishonest, but the Pardoner has a sense of humour with it, even suggesting that the dipping of the bone in the well can cure sexual jealousy. This direct look at his audience, with the innuendo that he knows their problems and can put them right, is followed by direct blackmail. He suggests that he *knows* the individual sinners in his audiences (of course he doesn't) and that he and only he can offer them absolution for their sins. Yet there is something disarming even about this, for he is admitting his practices openly to his *current* audience, the pilgrims. His boast of the hundred marks a year earned 'by this trick' is followed by a self-portrait which is a curious mixture of pride in his affectations and mockery of them. In a sense the Pardoner's prologue is his own confession of his own sins ('I preche of no-thing but for coveityse') but, as he is to discover, the Host at least resents his studied impertinence. He acknowledges that he does not care what happens to the souls of those he absolves, excuses himself by saying that sermons often spring from evil motives, and takes a pride in a kind of trade union of pardoners which operates a closed-shop beyond the reach of lay criticism. In effect he plays God, threatening anyone who has threatened the security of pardoners, and admits to his own hypocrisy, his seeming devout and truthful but exposing anyone he chooses to pick on. His admission that he preaches solely for greed is tinctured with the excuse that he can still make others repent for being greedy. This conceit in himself and in his office and function is despicable from the moral standpoint, yet his fluency is such that we can understand why audiences are taken in by him. He plays on the ignorant with his stories, despises those to whom he preaches, looks down on manual work, and has no compassion for the poor whom he delights in cheating. Yet it is an empty life. He boasts that he lives well and that he relishes having a pretty girl in every town, but we feel the pathos of the last boast. The Pardoner cannot 'have' girls; all that he has to live for is the good life of material possessions and gluttony (one of the sins he preaches against). The Prologue defines the man; the Tale establishes his techniques and skills, and exemplifies his professionalism in a degraded and degrading vocation.

The Pardoner is clever. He starts with the Tale and its setting, spells out the sins, and then turns to the examples which illustrate them. He keeps to his maxim that a good sermon can be built on an evil foundation. Drunkenness and gluttony are castigated, but the Pardoner himself is guilty of both – we remember that he required drink before addressing this particular audience. He is a fluent and accomplished speaker, incorporating quotations from the Bible and ancient writers in order to establish his full authority to judge sin as he does. This provides an insight into the man, so much so that we as readers respond to his condemnations and invocations despite the fact that we know they are being uttered by a despicable hypocrite. Even when he is inaccurate he compels a degree of admiration by his bravado. He can be coarse or, it seems, spiritually elevated, but we must remember that all of his voices are geared to the profit arising from successful sales-talk. In describing the mixing and diluting of wines he displays a somewhat acidic sense of humour; it is one swindler recognizing the cruder swindling of others.

The section on gambling illustrates the Pardoner's own gambling propensities. He is a gambler with words, hazarding examples, throwing rhetorical dice which he calculates will always show the right number willing to 'offer'. He is a snob who appeals to the inherent snobbery in others, citing examples of ambassadors and kings to impress the common and often ignorant people. His lack of real scriptural knowledge – or perhaps judgement is a better word – is shown in his indiscriminate 'placing' of sins, presenting swearing, for example, as being more culpable than murder. But his control of his audience and their responses is remarkable. He knows when to switch back from illustrations to the story which he only started at the beginning. There is cunning sleight of hand in this, for having drawn upon the religious examples his return to narrative whets the appetite of his listeners – and of his readers. And he proves that he can tell a story which is remarkable in terms of its speed and its conclusion, and which contains the mysterious figure of the old man, thus provoking his audience's speculation. In fact the Pardoner is laughing up his sleeve at the gullibility of his audience, and this is clear from the personification of Death and the simple equation of death with the gold. Just as the three revellers believe in the existence of 'a privee theef, men clepeth Deeth' – they are 'simple' – so they do not see, because of their wickedness, that the gold is death.

His handling of the actual story is brilliant. The learned references are temporarily in abeyance, and he reproduces the crisp colloquial dialogue which would be easily understood by his listeners. He is an actor who thus subtly varies the tone and emphasis of his own monologue by providing dramatic dialogue which stresses the moral immediacy for his audience. The conversations between the 'worst' of the three revellers and his companion which culminate in the determination to kill the third are balanced by the conversation between the youngest reveller and the chemist who supplies the poison which the youngest uses to kill the other two. The Pardoner then demonstrates that he is the master of anti-climax, almost discussing the deaths of the revellers as if they are no concern of his, a cunning way of telling his audience that if any of them go on sinning they will die. This throwaway approach is another form of blackmail. Those who do not wish to go on sinning will confess, pay money, and be absolved by the Pardoner. His profits will be ensured.

Again he turns back, the story being over, to the techniques he has employed earlier in his sermon, those of the learned reference and, more strongly, the rhetorical invocations against sin. Yet we are forced to wonder if the Pardoner truly knows himself, for after an appeal for money, goods from rings to wool and a promise to enter the saved souls on his list, he utters words which are likely to move his audience – the audience of pilgrims I mean – more profoundly than anything he has said. It is not a question of the Pardoner's sincerity or otherwise: it may be that he chooses the words because this is rather a different audience from the ones he is used to. Whatever the reason, they show a sensitivity to the moment which we should not have expected, and make us wonder whether beneath the professional actor, the grotesque man of fashion, there is a soul who knows that his own hope of salvation can only come with his own true confession. The words would be moving in any context, but they stand out here after the brazen acknowledgement of tricks, deception, greed:

And Iesu Crist, that is our soules leche,
So graunte yow his pardon to receyve;
For that is best; I wol yow nat deceyve.

It is a momentary insight, but the Pardoner quickly reverts to his concern for profit. It is almost as if these words slipped out before he could control them, that deep down there is a recognition of the true religion which his very practices undermine.

The result is that he now makes the most exaggerated of all his claims, and that is that his relics come from the Pope directly. There is little doubt that here he miscalculates or forgets the nature of this audience, for he offers opportunist absolution on the journey, even enjoying a rather malicious hope that someone will fall from his horse – in which case he will be saved provided that he pays. The moment of truth has been replaced by expectation of profit, as always, and in particularizing the Host the Pardoner makes another error of judgement. His neutered effeminacy invites the obvious obscenity of Harry Bailly. He is humiliated, too angry to reply. We have an uneasy feeling that this verbal bully is a physical coward, and that the reconciliation effected by the Knight has nothing of forgiveness in it on the Pardoner's part.

The presentation of the Pardoner is a masterly one, and other sections of this commentary will be devoted to Chaucer's narrative control, his irony and sense of structure. What is remarkable is the convincing nature of the portrait. We loathe the man but can't help admiring him; he is a rogue but a clever and successful one. He is a one-man show, having the skills of a ventriloquist, the insights of a psychologist and a kind of magnetic, if malign, power which keeps his listeners – and us – spellbound. He seems to have a compulsive need to confess what are his own sins to this new audience, and yet we do not feel that there is anything unnatural or unrealistic about this. By pushing his own malpractices he gains a hold over his audience, for such honesty carries with it its own reward. The reward is a ready ear, a fascination at the exposure of a sinner who is doing what he's urging them to do – confess. It is quite certain that the Pardoner loves the sound of his own voice, but what I am suggesting here is that he also enjoys a kind of masochistic display – it may compensate for his lack of sexuality – in which he puts himself into an unchallengeable position because he has already done what he is urging his audience to do – confess. The Pardoner is a hypocrite in terms of spiritual and religious practice, but essentially he tells the truth about his own hypocrisy.

The Pardoner claims to know his text by heart, and this leads to an interesting contemplation of his approach to this particular audience. Does he forget that audience for much of the time and just go through his prepared text? Or does he determine that he can get from this audience what he gets from his usual more ignorant audience? His success and prosperity depend on his ability and the extending of that ability. It seems to him that here he is accepting a challenge, fortified somewhat by drink, and that he exults in that challenge and its probable success until he is put down by the Host. The Pardoner is uncompromisingly aggressive. He cannot resist being centre stage, and we cannot resist the hypnotic quality of his performance.

The Church and the Pardoner

As we have noted, the Church played a dominating part in fourteenth-century life, and Chaucer in his work reflects many of its ideas and also the attitudes towards it held by his contemporaries. Not only did it provide employment for a large number of able members of the populace – who would probably have been professional men in another time – it was also one of the country's largest landowners. It therefore had a payroll of agricultural workers and labourers as well. The English Church was a branch of the Catholic Church, the two archbishops responsible for its organization in this country being those of York in the north and Canterbury in the south. The lesser bishops were responsible for the running of the churches throughout the country.

Just as Chaucer's focus in *The Canterbury Tales* generally is on the middle reaches of society, so in terms of religion in England his appraisal of Church practices and people embraces the middle range. In *The Canterbury Tales* the Prioress, the Monk, the Friar, the Parson, the Summoner and the Pardoner indicate the range of ecclesiastics – and Church auxiliaries – covered by Chaucer. Chaucer's own emphasis here is a sharp one, for these representatives of various facets of the Church's work are strongly individualized.

The Church's main function was to promote Christian principles and practice. It existed to save souls through the sacraments – the Mass in particular. Medieval plays inevitably had religious subjects and Christian morality as their themes, hence their being known as miracle or morality plays. The people and the church were also closely associated in the social sense. The community sometimes arranged banquets inside the church and dances in the churchyard. Although these activities were criticized – and in this period the Church often criticized itself – it once more demonstrates the centrality of the Church in medieval life, reflecting a sense of community and participation in the nine thousand or so churches scattered throughout England.

The Pope was the leader of the Church, though in the fourteenth century (which was the time of the Great Schism) there was another claimant to the title who set out his opposition at Avignon in France. Two centuries later England was to break free from the Catholic Church, but in the fourteenth century during this controversy England remained loyal to the Pope in Rome. The Pope appointed the bishops, and sent out the friars and pardoners to each country which owed religious allegiance to Rome. These bishops were often men of high talent but not necessarily very devout, able administrators rather than men of great dedication. Some were foreign, some were frequently or permanently absent from their allotted area, and the result was that the fourteenth century witnessed displays of anti-episcopal feeling as administrative responsibilities devolved upon archdeacons, deans and canons of cathedral chapters, who resented undertaking a work-load which properly belonged to their bishop.

Another important aspect of Church organization was the monastery with an established order of monks, who prayed, worked and even did the manual labour of the fields. Sometimes these monasteries were rich, with outlying 'cells' which had to be visited and inspected. (Note the reference to one such 'cell' at Roncevalles in the description of the Pardoner in the *General Prologue*.) Monks at this time often led corrupt and worldly lives as a result of laxity in the observation of the monastic forms and the increased freedom obtained from the 'cells'. Yet some of the orders were strict, devout, meticulous in their practices and their self-denial. Chaucer's Monk is one of the former, loose-living, enjoying his food and hunting, worldly. It is noticeable in the Prologue to *The Canterbury Tales* and in *The Pardoner's Tale* that Chaucer is intent on attacking the worldliness of the Church and the corruption of some of her servants. In this he would be voicing what was largely the popular opinion of the time. In no way could such criticism be interpreted as reflecting any lack of faith on Chaucer's part.

The friars, of which there were four orders, came from Rome. They were assigned to a certain district in which they could beg for their order. Although they were often the best preachers, they were not popular. Chaucer obviously shared the largely common dislike of them, hence his portrait in the Prologue of the Friar, Hubert. The friars acted as confessors and often granted absolution, thus undermining the church, for the local priest did not always have this power. They represented another aspect of the worldliness of the Church.

Nuns tended to come from a courtly background, the superior social class, and this meant that the convents of the time often reflected the refinement and elegance of these ladies. They relieved the sick and the poor, but were often not especially religious themselves, being given to good works but rather removed from life experience. It is in the character of the country Parson that Chaucer presents the member of the Church who would be seen by the common people. Usually such a man would be very poorly paid for his work. He had to say Mass, preach sermons, absolve sins as well as undertaking marriage and baptismal services. Chaucer's Parson in the Prologue is idealized. He is a scholar, a man who is gentle and relenting. He would not insist that those who didn't pay tithes (one-tenth of each man's revenue) were punished if they were poor. He is restrained in dealing with confessions, and sought 'To drawen folk to heven by fairnesse'. The Parson had a clerk as his assistant, who would be in possession of a salary. The Clerk from Oxford in the Prologue is intent on study and is very poor and unworldly.

The Summoner and the Pardoner are very much of their time. Since the Church in England accepted the Roman Canon Law (ecclesiastical law as laid down in decrees of the Pope and statutes of Ecclesiastical Councils), and added its own laws to it where they were needed, it had to be enforced by church officers, chief of whom would be the archdeacon in every diocese. He had great powers, the greatest being that of excommunication. This was the Pope's power to exclude someone from the Church sacraments. In effect it meant banishment from the Catholic Church. Clerics guilty of breaking the law were tried in Church courts, and such sins as witchcraft or perjury or sexual immorality were naturally thought to be more serious in a cleric than in a layman. In these instances the archdeacons were called upon to pronounce punishment. Archdeacons, deacons and summoners were all open to bribes, and there was a great deal of criticism of them and hatred for them. It was the summoner's task to bring before the ecclesiastical court anyone charged with an offence, and certainly Chaucer's Summoner is seen unsympathetically both physically and mentally. He knows everyone's business, takes bribes and guarantees freedom in return, provided that he is plied with money. Summoners had much legal grafting to do. They were often ill-educated and did not understand what they were about. The position almost invited abuse, but once again much of the responsibility for that must be laid at the door of the Church. The scholar John of Salisbury is quoted as saying of summoners 'Their high office makes it their duty to keep God's Law, yet they keep it not', an indication that the Church could not control an important employee.

That statement is certainly true of the pardoners. The medieval pardoner or *quaester* was empowered to travel from the Papal Court in order to sell indulgences, to offer relics and to preach sermons against the deadly sins (indulgences involved a remission of the temporal punishment for sin after the guilt has been forgiven). The Church taught that after the forgiveness of sin there was still a degree of working repentance to be completed here or in the after-life. Obviously prayers were one means of doing this, but it also became the practice to give money which would be devoted to the use of the Church. One sees where the corruption began and why. Simple people began to believe that the forgiveness of God could be bought, that spending money was preferable to fasting, that the pardoner had special powers, while the pardoner became a kind of spiritual tax-collector who could so easily line his own pockets. True repentance tended to be overlooked in what had become a financial bargain.

Pardoners could either be laymen or priests. Chaucer's Pardoner would appear to be a layman, judging from his attention to fashion and his lank locks, which show that he did not have a tonsured head. Pardoners frequently made extravagant claims for their powers and functions. A racket grew up in relics and pardons, so much so that Pope Boniface IX condemned the practices of many pardoners in 1390. Once again the Church, in giving pardoners an accredited position and role, had started something which could not be successfully brought within their disciplines. Pardoners, like summoners, became a focal point of criticism and hatred, and inevitably the Church drew upon itself a share of both for allowing these areas of corruption to continue without positive challenge. Given the right of entry to parish churches in order to preach – as the prelude to selling – the pardoner could of course undermine the practice of the priest. Maurice Hussey has put quite succinctly Chaucer's conception of the Summoner and the Pardoner in the Prologue and the way in which we should see them:

They were despicable as individuals, but institutionally they had the power of summoning and in many cases of absolving or pardoning lay folk. On a small scale they seem to act out the summoning of all mankind to judgement on the Last Day . . . Both men are shown to us as sick men, hysterical and a little mad, and this we should interpret in both the spiritual and physical sense.

It was impossible for the Church to control them because of poor communications, and it is certainly true to say that they were abhorred and reviled and yet of course contributed to Church funds, ironically helping to provide new churches through what they were doing. This may be why it was so long (1562) before the office of pardoner was officially abolished by the Church.

Themes and Morality

Both these are sufficiently clear on a close reading of *The Pardoner's Tale*. The theme is succinctly stated by the Pardoner as being 'For the love of money is the root of all evil', but it would be a mistake to consider this as the only theme, and in any case it is a set-piece of the Pardoner's. He also attacks gluttony, drunkenness, gambling, the swearing of oaths and the taking of the Lord's name in vain whether casually or as a passionate curse. Thus the themes of the tale become all these, with greed at the top of the list, since possession of money means that man has the wherewithal to practise the sins he most wishes to, as the revellers freely admit. The themes are emphasized by reference to the Bible or to the instances of great men to support them. The overt theme is the preaching against sin, the irony being that the preacher is himself a practitioner of the sins he preaches against.

The Pardoner's Tale reflects Chaucer's own morality which, by showing us the Pardoner in action, is making a comment on him, his practices, the Church, man and Christianity. Hypocrisy and deception are at the centre of the moral attack, but there is also an area which consists of a castigation of the Pardoner for being unscrupulous, for taking advantage of the poor, for claiming to be what he is not, for practising the sins that he preaches against, and most notably, the one which forms the main theme of his text. For the Pardoner is guilty of believing that to preach that money is the root of all evil is enough, since people will repent, though he himself will not and will continue his practices, his devices and the selling of his fakes. The moral theme of the Pardoner's tale is therefore by implication a support for the precepts and practice of Christianity. The old man is a good example. He cites the Bible in support of the moral standpoint that respect should be shown to old age. The boy servant naïvely telling the revellers that they should beware of death according to what his mother has told him in the past is in fact saying (though he doesn't know it) that one should reject temptation, greed, self-indulgence, all of which constitute the rule of a moral death. It will be noted that each of the revellers – as well as the Pardoner himself– is completely selfish. If Chaucer is attacking the morality of the Church he is doing so in the person of the Pardoner, indicating that such a person is a disgrace to a Church which is based on the principles, example and teaching of Christ. Yet such is Chaucer's tone that we marvel at the fine degree of tolerance he shows. He even gives the Pardoner three lines (588–90) which exemplify the Christian message and the fact that it has got *through* to him, transcending his own petty practice. And next to the word 'morality' one must place the words 'wisdom' and 'humour'. Only a man with a richly comic sense could have the Pardoner confess, then try to take advantage of the audience he has confessed to, and follow this with the Host coarsely upbraiding the Pardoner in earthy language which provokes in us a smile or laugh of agreement. And only a wise man rich in life experience could present this unattractive and hypocritical man in such a way as to draw from us not only condemnation but also a kind of understanding, an appreciation that it does indeed take all kinds of people to make the variety of life. The pilgrims are a microcosm of medieval society, and this allows a criminal and corrupt Church subordinate like the Pardoner to be reconciled to the Host through the pious and noble offices of the Knight. In effect it shows a high moral idealism, a wisdom which sees strife as degrading and mutual acceptance in generosity of spirit as sublime.

Chaucer's Art in The Pardoner's Tale

INTRODUCTION

One of the most remarkable facets of Chaucer's art in *The Pardoner's Tale* (including the Prologue to it) is his ability to combine realistic detail on the one hand with allusive and learned reference on the other. It is high art to achieve a successful blend yet here, as in *The Wife of Bath's Tale*, the learning and observation which are Chaucer's do not detract from our appreciation of the Tale nor do they undermine the credibility of the teller, whether it be the Wife or the Pardoner. The result of this blend is that Chaucer is able to project the personality of the teller (and make voiced and unvoiced comments on that teller) and at the same time to employ technical and imaginative devices which enhance the Tale.

THE SERMON

The Pardoner's Tale is a sermon, and because of the character of the teller and his practices, a black parody of a sermon at the same time. Medieval sermons involved an elaborate theory of preaching, and a set of rules, and treatises were written setting out their form. Many were complex, but in the main they had six divisions, the first being a definition of the main theme, the second a general introductory section related to the theme, followed by a close examination of the original text or theme. The fourth section would be an illustrative story or anecdote of the theme (an *exemplum*). The last sections covered the application of the teaching and the blessing of the audience. The preacher himself represents the voice of God, whom he must praise, and the aim of the sermon is to improve the minds of the audience and to direct them towards prayer and Christian activity. You will see from this – and this is a bare summary of the complexity of medieval sermons, which A. C. Spearing has said were often 'a public meditation on the original text with a structure as complex as that of a sonata or a symphony' – why I described the Pardoner's perversion of the sermon as a 'black parody'. What Chaucer does is to take some of the preacher's techniques and some aspects of the sermon pattern, giving to both the highly individual twists which fit the minds of this professional twister.

The theme is stated in the Prologue, but although the biblical references support the theme, the Pardoner also uses examples from secular writers and from contemporary life. The biblical references are, on one or two occasions, not quite accurate, and perhaps this too reflects the fact that the Pardoner is not quite of the Church though claiming to have its authority.

THE PARDONER'S PROLOGUE

Other aspects of the Prologue merit close attention as indicating Chaucer's art in making the Pardoner's sales-talk effective, even though it is a compound of blackmail and boasting. The blackmail is seen in the Pardoner's refusal to absolve anyone who admits to having committed a terrible sin. This is sound, establishing the determination of the Pardoner to get everything he can from his audience. All that needs to be said here is that no one is likely to admit to major sin publicly, and this means that anyone is free to make offerings to the Pardoner, which is just what he desires. In part of this address he is ingratiating, putting himself on a good footing with his typical audience. But now he turns aside to the atypical audience before him and boasts of how much he earns. The statement exemplifies his theme – 'For the love of money is the root of all evil' – and as such it is the root of the Pardoner's own evil practices.

VARIETY OF LANGUAGE

Already the variety of language is apparent in *The Pardoner's Prologue.* One of the brilliant Chaucerian devices here is to have the
Pardoner stand off and look at himself. From his standing 'lyk a
clerk in my pulpet' the Pardoner is consciously contemplating himself, watching his own performance with the admiring eye of
someone who knows that he is good. Yet the language is revealing.
The reference to the 'clerk' is interesting, since the clerk would be
salaried but official within the Church, whereas the Pardoner has
to get what he gets and feels himself outside the main Church ethos
(though of course claiming to have all kinds of authority from the
Pope downwards). There is of course a mockery in the tone, a
knock at propriety and officialdom which shows the worldliness of
the Pardoner. His stretching forth of his neck and turning himself
about is in fact unconscious self-caricature. Chaucer has achieved
two things here. He has first shown the Pardoner's pride in being
the focus of attention, yet by subtle description within the Pardoner's own viewing of himself we know that Chaucer is mocking
him, seeing his gestures as exaggerated and emanating from performance and not sincerity. As so often in the Tale, Chaucer has the
Pardoner choose an image from nature to exemplify his attitude or
his practice. Here the reference to 'a dowve sitting on a berne' also
has the two-fold effect which we have noticed above. The movement of a dove's head has a certain to-ing and fro-ing, almost mecha-
nistic quality, so that this too is a kind of subtle mockery of the
Pardoner's gestures through an innocent-seeming image. And that
image carries associations for contemporary readers, one of Chaucer's typical country images but here having perhaps a spiritual
overtone. If so it would be an ironic one, for the dove stands for
the Holy Ghost in the Trinity. We have indicated that this is a
black parody of a sermon, and it is references like this which maintain this effect.

The Pardoner in performance is full of nervous energy, delighting
in his own greed which underpins the story of greed to come. The
mocking reference to the clerk is followed by a catalogue of his (the
Pardoner's) own unclerical and unspiritual qualities which have
nothing to do with 'correccioun of sinne'. The statements are redolent

of daring and bravado, almost as if the Pardoner is enjoying *exposing* himself for what he is to this rather different audience. The climax of his audacity is shown in the lines

> I rekke never, whan that they ben beried,
> Though that her soules goon a-blakeberied!

We note another image from nature – to people living largely on the land – as a stress-mark of the Pardoner's lack of concern. The people of his time would pick blackberries as a way of eking out what in many cases would be a very poor subsistence. By analogy the Pardoner is always after more substantial 'pickings', and his comfortable subsistence contrasts with that of the poor.

OTHER IMAGES

Two other metaphors used by the Pardoner in his prologue are worthy of note. Again it would seem that Chaucer's language is very carefully chosen, and that it may have biblical associations of which the Pardoner is unaware. The first is his assertion 'Than wol I stinge him with my tonge smerte' and 'Thus spitte I out my venim under hewe/Of holynesse, to seme holy and trewe'. The snake reference is close to that of the serpent and the tempting of Eve, and it is true that the Pardoner is a tempter and, moreover, that his practices are devilish and far from holy. With the structure of the Tale in mind, we might note that this is spiritual poisoning which finds an echo in the actual poisoning within the tale itself. He tempts with the offer of heaven, and his language and its promise are as spurious as the serpent's offer of godlike status to Adam and Eve. The Chaucerian irony plays over these images, for the Pardoner, who relies on his biblical authority to win his audience, is unwittingly setting up a biblical association which underlines his own damnation.

This leads logically to a consideration of the Pardoner as a great twister of words and morals in the next section of the Prologue. Though he is guilty of greed himself, he says,

> Yet can I maken other folk to twinne
> From avaryce, and sore to repente.

We should look closely at this, for at the end of his Prologue the Pardoner reiterates it in a slightly different form – 'For, though myself be a ful vicious man . . .' Now this in effect is the Pardoner justifying himself, and making sure that he has the best of both worlds. He is saying that the ends justify the means – but he is also saying that the means justify the ends. This is typical of his duplicity, but what we are aware of is that *the moral content* of any tale he may tell may still be effective despite his confession. We can take it that the Pardoner does not confess to his usual audience, but this has the effect of making things worse. Confessions and money and goods to someone who is fundamentally dishonest and hypocritical and concerned only with self can have no spiritual value. By revealing himself here in this way the Pardoner is employing corruption which was not sanctioned by the Church although that Church undoubtedly knew that it was going on. These abuses are thus being exposed by Chaucer through his creature, and almost certainly, as Spearing points out, Chaucer would be aware of Pope Boniface's letter of 1390 in which he refers to the number of fake pardoners who claim to have been authorized by the papal officers to 'receive money for us and the Roman Church, and they go about the country under these pretexts'. This is just the Pardoner's stance. The bad man parodies the good sermon, yet goodness can come out of this evil, though the lining of the Pardoner's pockets may well be filled.

MORAL IRONY

Chaucer's keen social and moral eye further exposes the Pardoner towards the end of the latter's Prologue. The term would not be current in Chaucer's time, but there is little doubt that because he believes in the image he is projecting, the Pardoner is a snob. In the first instance, he looks down on the people to whom he preaches (see the section on *Sin* in this commentary). There is a sneer of contempt in the assertion

> For lewed peple loven tales olde;
> Swich thinges can they wel reporte and holde.

And once again I suggest that this shows Chaucer working at his customary depth, for the Pardoner's own practice is related to this statement. He too loves (or rather uses) the proven tales which he himself can retain (he admits to learning by heart). He too can 'wel reporte and holde', in fact it is his stock-in-trade, his basic repertoire, the means he employs to further his own mercenary ends, for the Pardoner is assuredly a spiritual mercenary. Thus Chaucer is linking the Pardoner with those he dupes. He looks down on them because of their limitations; he himself is circumscribed by similar limitations. The irony is that his are turned to gain, theirs to credulous acceptance of the ham actor before them whose script never varies, whose performance is word-perfect, whose mask is sincerity and whose practice is sin.

A further aspect of the Pardoner's snobbery and immorality is seen in his refusal to do manual labour and, thus exemplifying the sin of sloth which he condemns, his rejection of poverty (which was often associated with the Christian faith in medieval times). He has faith, faith in his ability to beg in 'sondry londes' (an indication of the importance of travel in his time) and a determination to let nothing stand in his way of having 'money, wolle, chese, and whete'. He expresses a callous indifference to starvation (again we are reminded of the low subsistence level of so many of the population in this period) and it is this heartlessness *before* the actual sermon begins which alienates us and, doubtless, most of the audience of pilgrims. The repetition of the word 'povrest' contrasted with the lush single-word effects of having plenty is most effective, and leaves us in no doubt where Chaucer's own sympathies lie. The 'Joly wenche in every toun' strikes the one pathetic note. The Pardoner, deprived of sexuality, lays claim to possessing it. He doesn't, but compensates by embracing fully the other sins of the flesh he condemns.

The main *exemplum* of the Tale is of course the story of the search after Death, which keeps to the sermon tradition. This is followed by his comments on the story and, before the altercation with the Host, a parody of the blessing by the sharp display of the relics and the offer to absolve anyone who accidentally falls off his horse and injures himself. But before that there is a moment which approximates to a blessing ('And Iesu Crist, that is our soules leche . . .'), so that one is left with the distinct impression that Chaucer has used in outline the structure of the sermon, employing variety and different emphases in this adaptation to suit the character of the Pardoner. This is in no sense a criticism of the Church – the whole tale is a criticism of the malpractices of pardoners – nor is it satirical. It is a clever way of appealing to an audience and at the same time conveying the appeal of the Pardoner to his audiences. We must remember that in the Middle Ages and after the sermon was one of the most popular forms of communication, and this particularly applies before the age of printing (Caxton printed the first book in England in 1477). But because of the medieval emphasis on the structure of the sermon, it becomes one of the major literary genres, orally received and appreciated in Chaucer's time, and later, up to the Reformation and beyond, forming perhaps the major part of devotional literature. Chaucer through the Pardoner's brilliant adaptation transformed the form to his own particular moral needs; the preacher stands condemned out of his own mouth, having used the form which should echo the word of God.

NARRATIVE ART

Economy

If the medieval sermon provides Chaucer with the basic structure for *The Pardoner's Tale*, the actual techniques and language of the Pardoner provide us with further insights into the subtlety and variety of Chaucer's art. The Pardoner employs the preaching technique of a list of examples, balancing the statement with an anecdote which illustrates it. But what he also does is to vary his voice according to the material he is using. I have said elsewhere (p. 114) that he is an actor, and the whole sequence from the Prologue to the end is really a histrionic performance. A close look at the Prologue to the Tale and the Tale itself will indicate the variety. If we take the first six lines of the Prologue we see the Pardoner's superb sense of *economy*. Into those six lines he manages to get (a) his preaching method: the technique of knowing what he is going to say by heart and uttering it in a suitably varied voice and tone to impress his audience; (b) an image –

that of the bell – which will be picked up later and which has resonances within the Tale itself, for the revellers hear the bell which signifies the burial of the corpse and which is also ironically the beginning of their quest for death. It leads to their own deaths. This is not all. The Pardoner tells us that the revellers were drinking in a tavern 'Longe erst er pryme rong of any belle', a direct reference to a religious observance which they do not follow and which they blaspheme by their actions. This demonstrates Chaucer's sense of the structure of his tale in the detail as well as in the mass; and (c) he spells out his theme, which has the dual relevance of being his own motive and a cautionary tale to his audience not to practise what he himself lives for. I have deliberately selected this example because it indicates Chaucer's art. The Tale is so tightly constructed that no words are wasted and, as we shall see later, even the Pardoner's apparent verbosity has its own emotive influence on the audience.

Language

The reader will note the immediacy of the Tale's opening, the truism that a good story must have a good beginning. Having established this, we note the variety of the techniques employed by Chaucer in the form of the Pardoner's language. We have noted that the Pardoner has the skills of a ventriloquist. These skills are exemplified in the Prologue to the Tale, where he sets forth his spurious spiritual stall complete with bulls and relics. The language is factual, for the Pardoner wants to impress the facts of his authority, but even here the language used shows us how *inside* his man Chaucer is. The image from cookery is a good example: 'To saffron with my predicacioun' is not only relevant to the gluttony which the Pardoner is condemning, but a direct indication of the way he thinks. The metaphor reflects his own gluttony, his intention to lead the good life in terms of food and drink which his 'gluttony' for money and goods will provide. It is linked to another aspect of the language too – the fascination the Pardoner has for what is foul and diseased, from the 'pokkes and of scabbe, and every sore' in sheep to the 'O stinking cod,/Fulfild of donge and of corrupcioun!' of bodily function. It is almost as if this obsession with the unpleasant aspects of the flesh is a moral indicator to his obsession with the diseased aspects of the spirit – sin, both in himself and in others. Chaucer extends his coarseness in this area by complementing it with the coarseness of the Host in his direct and outspoken rejection of the Pardoner's invitation.

Techniques

Evidence of the packed nature of the language is abundant. An image like 'To kindle and blowe the fyr of lecherye' is evocative of hell-fire, and the revellers are assuredly destined for a medieval hell. It is consonant with what I might call the biblical emphasis in the Prologue, with the examples of Lot and Herod, the latter somewhat distorted. There is little doubt that this is deliberate on Chaucer's part. The sinful Pardoner is guilty of inaccuracy, but since he is a fake anyway such inaccuracy is to be expected. The reference to Seneca seems to indicate the Pardoner's range, but in fact it provides him with the opportunity to use one of his favourite devices before returning to the Bible and citing the example of Adam. I refer to the apostrophizing which is calculated to raise the temperature of the audience, the rhetorical and repetitive mode which has always been the stand-by of the preacher or the man with a message;

> O glotonye, ful of cursednesse,
> O cause first of our confusioun,
> O original of our dampnacioun . . .

The exclamations are imbued with passion, even if it is an actor's passion. And once again a close look demonstrates just how clever it is, just how carefully the sequence is being followed to produce the maximum effect. Look at 'cause first' and 'original', and you see immediately why it is being repeated for emphasis. The reason is that the 'cause first' goes back indeed to the 'original' – Adam himself, the first man. We may wonder at the choice of Adam as an instance of gluttony, and indeed although Chaucer would have read of this idea, it may well be that he is laughing at it too and thus again showing the individuality of the Pardoner's examples. But for the Pardoner it is the demonstration of his method, for from Adam the first of men he takes the natural step of condemning contemporary men for continuing the practice of gluttony for which the first man was condemned.

Contrast and Sounds

There follows an effective use of contrast, something at which the Pardoner and his creator are adept. Two references to St Paul by way of biblical support for his theme are embedded in the description, so to speak, of the 'ends' of gluttony, the exquisite 'the shorte throte, the tendre mouth' being followed by the far-ranging search for food and drink for the 'glotoun', and climaxed by the unequivocal assertion that too much drink makes a man's throat 'his privee'. All the while we are aware of the irony, for the Pardoner in describing the indulgence is creating the sensations – the pleasure of food and the disgust of excess. And once launched on these themes the Pardoner proceeds to elaborate them by employing an even greater use of contrast. The 'apostel weping' gives him a chance to display his own capacity for tears of sadness at the contemplation of wicked man (perhaps even himself included). But with a typical transition to another mood – and the Pardoner is a master of moods – he proceeds to another invocatory damnation of the 'stinking cod', ending his attack on gluttony with another resonance that equates moral death with the Death of the story to come:

> But certes, he that haunteth swich delyces
> Is deed, whyl that he liveth in tho vyces.

The couplet rounds off superbly and with finality a condemnation which is remarkable for the variety of language employed, and again there is a lead into the next section. The link is the deliberate effect produced by the sounds of certain words and phrases. Take a phrase like 'the golet softe and swote', where the hard 'g' sound can almost be equated with the gulp, the greed of swallowing. It is cleverly balanced by the actual smooth passage of the food, the alliterative 'softe and swote' of soft 's' and harder 't' sounds conveying the actual process of pleasure in taste. But in the section which follows the alliteration has been replaced by onomatopoeia, the sounds of drunken breathing conveyed by the word 'Sampsoun'. This again shows Chaucer working at some depth, because the name of Samson is associated with abstemiousness (thus this is a form of irony) and it enables the Pardoner, so to speak, to combine an example and a fact. The irony is further compounded because Samson was renowned for his physical strength whereas the drunken man has palpably lost his. This use of sounds – and it runs through the Tale – contains an appeal to the senses, one delightful, one revolting, with the corollary that the one becomes the other once we indulge to excess. The Pardoner can both woo and bludgeon his audience through the sounds and suggestions of the words he chooses.

Humour

Having used biblical illustrations the Pardoner again varies his approach to his audience, this time displaying a drily ironic sense of humour as he refers to another contemporary malpractice. I refer to the diluting of a good wine with a cheap one, practical deception which matches the Pardoner's own spiritual deception and indeed has the same end – commercial profit. It is a tongue-in-cheek reference, an oblique acknowledgement of the success of other rogues:

> This wyn of Spayne crepeth subtilly
> In othere wynes, growing faste by . . .

It would not be lost on an audience of pilgrims nor, one suspects, on some members of a rustic audience. A further biblical reference follows this joke before the Pardoner proceeds to his attack on gambling, and here there is yet another variation.

Relevance

The lead up to what we may call the gambling sequence is characterized by the subtlety we have now come to expect. This sequence is comparatively short (see the note in the *Structural Summary*), and the instances cited in support are not biblical, though they demonstrate the range of the Pardoner's supposed reading. Before these illustrations the catalogue of crimes traceable to gambling proves to be a somewhat indiscriminate one. This is a failing of the Pardoner's – it shows the essentially superficial level at which he operates – a failing which is repeated in the next section on swearing, which he ranks more seriously than he does murder. In fact in his list he ends with something of an anti-climax, saying that gambling is a waste of time and goods. Yet the fact is that the list includes treachery, blasphemy and murder, all directly relevant to the coming story of the revellers who, we remember, were described at the very beginning of the Tale as gamblers who 'pleye at dees bothe day and night'. This looks forward in fact to the 'gamble' of the three men in the story. They gamble on finding Death and killing him but, best of all, two gamble to kill the third, who in turn gambles on two of his three bottles being able to kill his two companions. If you like, the odds in each case are two to one and, another ironic stroke, the two revellers have the high ambition after their murder of being able to 'pleye at dees right at our owene wille'.

After this introduction another aspect of the Pardoner's technique – and of Chaucer's art in his understanding of human nature – is shown by the choice of illustrations, which are calculated to appeal to the inherent snobbery of the Pardoner's listeners. And I believe that in this instance the Pardoner has the particular audience of pilgrims in mind. He refers to status, and then produces the two examples of Stilbon's visit to find his potential allies great gamblers, following this up with the story of the King of the Parthians and Demetrius. The brevity of the treatment is not dismissive. Rather it focuses on the sin of gambling in high places which might be calculated to move an audience markedly aware of status and indeed having people of high status in it. The examples are likely to make the audience admire the Pardoner. He is cleverly being radical and conservative at the same time, condemning gambling among kings and urging his audience to demonstrate that they do not embrace the same vice. Again the concluding couplet of this section is effective, expressive of tolerance and a kind of wisdom:

> Lordes may finden other maner pley
> Honeste y-nough to dryve the day awey.

I have already referred to the fact that the Pardoner places swearing above murder in his catalogue of sins. This is Chaucer's subtle way of indicating that the Pardoner's priorities are wrong ones, but it is also an ironic look at the gullibility of the audience and at medieval value judgements, with the oath thought of as the tearing of Christ's body. Having spelled out the evil, the Pardoner proceeds to quote oaths. The relevance of two lines in particular to the story is quite apparent. They are what I would call the forecasting element in

Chaucer, the implanting of an idea or picture in the reader's mind before it actually occurs. The lines are:

> '. . . By goddes armes, if thou falsly pleye,
> This dagger shal thurgh-out thyn herte go'

The context is a gambling scene, but it is a scene which we are shortly to witness – the stabbing of the youngest reveller according to plan, after all three have played falsely.

Tension and Realism

The story itself is high narrative art – it is packed with tension, economically and hence dramatically immediate, and there is a sense of realism too. Hitherto we have considered Chaucer's artistic presentation of the Pardoner's monologue, but the tale carries a related though different emphasis. We have already referred to the ringing of the bell and its immediate associations in the context of the story. That is the artist showing literary awareness.

But one of Chaucer's main achievements in the tale itself is his ability to convey realism in character through dialogue. One of the revellers asks about the corpse. The reply from his servant is ingenuous and direct – briefly he says that it was one of their old companions who was dead drunk and who was slain by 'a privee theef, men clepeth Deeth'. The boy's words are natural, unaffected, real. He mentions the current plague casually, he tells of the silence of Death, he warns them to be ready to meet Death, and he concludes with the simple but moving 'Thus taughte me my dame'. The effect on the attentive reader is immediate. The boy represents an innocent and literal way of life in the midst of corruption. The publican refers to him as a child. Yet unwittingly this child has set the action in motion, and the first reveller to speak blasphemes three times against God *and* urges the swearing of the blood brotherhood oath which all three are so soon to break. The language is as crisp and immediate as the motivation to kill Death. Phrases like 'I shal him seke by wey and eek by strete', 'we three been al ones' and 'He shal be slayn, which that so many sleeth' convey the excitement of the reveller, the swift determination *and* the literary craftsmanship of the author. The author is cunning, for in the next paragraph we are told that the revellers are in a drunken rage, which hardly makes for the clarity of utterance we have seen above. But the words occur before the commentary and they condition our response.

The Old Man

The meeting with the old man is the crucial point in the story. If the child provides the script then the old man is the producer and director, for he directs them to the gold and this inevitably, and predictably, produces the results. I have said in the note on p. 77 of this commentary that the old man represents goodness and wisdom. Of course he represents much more than that and has, in fact, been a focal point of critical interpretation. Here, with the usual convincing dialogue, there is interaction between the old man, who is poor and humble, and the revellers ('al dronken') aggressive and rude. The old man has his roots in folk-lore, but Chaucer's presentation of him is individual and mystical. He is not just a caricature or symbol. We get the impression of individuality, particularly when he 'gan loke in his visage', because we feel that he is looking into the very *soul* of the reveller. We note the obvious contrast between youth and age, but it is age which has already been with him too long. The contrast is further explored by Chaucer, for the old man wishes to die but cannot, the revellers wish to kill Death but cannot. Yet what Chaucer is representing is a kind of Christian resignation; the old man must suffer although he is good, for genuine Christianity is compounded of humility, resignation and suffering. The old man therefore exists on two levels in this tale – a real old man who stands in contrast to the revellers, and a figure representative of Christian wisdom and endurance whose journey towards death is not completed. The splendid irony of his presentation is that the Pardoner is showing a pilgrim to the pilgrims, a figure who will impress them by his own virtues.

The account of the old man has a curiously poignant emphasis. The personification of the earth as his mother conveys a tremulous immediacy and, as with the child, one feels a sense of innocence and incorruptibility. It is doubtless part of Chaucer's narrative method to point up this contrast for, as I have said earlier in this section, both the old man and the child have a *function* in the story. The pathos of the old man's appeal, however, gives way to a sterner attitude towards the revellers for the way they have spoken to him. It is almost as if he is an Old Testament Patriarch rebuking an errant member of the tribe. His citing of biblical authority about the respect to be shown to the old strikes a genuine Christian note by contrast with the Pardoner's studied references which are merely oiling the wheels of profit. The structural depth is apparent. The Pardoner cites the Bible publicly, the old man cites the Bible in the Tale – his authority reinforces his own miniature sermon. The contrast continues to be felt, for just as the Pardoner directs his audience towards gain for himself, so the old man directs the revellers towards gain for themselves, and both kinds of 'gain' are death – moral and spiritual in the case of the Pardoner, physical in the case of the revellers. And at the same time, in the true Christian spirit, the old man invokes the name of God in blessing and not in blasphemy – 'And god be with yow, wher ye go or ryde.'

In convincing dialogue the youth and age contrast continues, and we note the simplicity and the effective repetition. The reveller in altercation with the old man swears four times, he uses the word 'trouthe' which was pledged in the blood brotherhood, and he calls the old man 'thou false theef!' which reminds us of the boy's description of 'a privee theef, men clepeth Deeth'. Now this last reference adds a mystical dimension to the old man. If he is not Death, he directs men to death. And he does so immediately after the accusation that he is Death's spy. Even his direction is tempered by a blessing, though the 'croked wey' is a simple means of indicating the moral direction in which the revellers are going. The folk-tale element, with its clear natural description, is very evident at this stage. Once more we note the economy. As soon as the old man has directed them, the revellers reach the tree and the treasure. This occupies four lines, the fifth being the superbly ironic 'No lenger thanne after Deeth they soughte'. Thanks to the old man they have found it. Fable, realism Christianity, retribution are all successfully blended. The old man, however, continues his search (and we are mindful of it) for death.

THE REVELLERS: CHARACTERIZATION

'The worste of hem' takes over. He preaches on the cunning theme of
acquisition, revealing a sharp intelligence (as he himself boasts) which
is something akin to the Pardoner's. It is a crooked scheme but the
narrative is wonderfully crisp and straightforward, carrying the action
from the plan of the youngest one leaving to the next plan, the
doublecrossing of the youngest. Even in the unfolding of this plan
there is some subtlety of characterization, for the planner is clever
and devious, his companion rather unintelligent, or perhaps too drunk
to understand what is being proposed until it is spelled out to him.
The dialogue is natural, unforced, direct. One line, perhaps, has
Christian associations, for 'And I shal ryve him thurgh the sydes
tweye' suggests the thrusting of the spear into Christ on the cross.
The youngest who is to be so treated cannot be seen as Christ, but
just as the Pardoner's sermon is a black parody so this has the same
kind of effect, a perversion of an aspect of the crucifixion by those
who are leading perverted and evil lives.

So strong is the sense of structural balance in the tale that as this
plan is being concocted so the youngest concocts his own. The implicit
suggestion is that evil living breeds corruption of the mind and heart,
direct evidence as far as the Pardoner is concerned of the truth of his
preaching. In effect the youngest's plan is spelled out briefly and the
technique employed is analogous to the twentieth-century stream of
consciousness technique employed by writers like James Joyce; the
words are only spoken aloud in the narrative because it is essential
that the audience hear the thoughts spoken for dramatic effect.
The Pardoner himself interrupts his Tale, though not formally, playing omniscient author in order to stress the fact that the Devil has
been able to seduce him (the youngest) because of his wicked way of
life. It is an interjection to remind the audience of his theme before
they get carried away on the next wave of expectation.

ANIMAL AND NATURAL ASSOCIATIONS

Once the youngest goes to the chemist we note the use of animal examples which inevitably reflect on the reveller and his companions, who are the 'vermin' and 'rattes' of society. The excuse for buying the poison is transparent to us because already admitted, but convincing in context, and it provides an example of another Chaucerian character cameo. The chemist, like the Pardoner, is a salesman and, like the Pardoner, a super salesman if his assessment of his own goods is anything to go by. He requires a mere nine lines to testify to the efficacy of the poison; it is so strong that 'Noght but the mountance of a corn of whete' is needed to kill a man. The natural imagery enhances the effect of the unnatural action.

NARRATIVE PACE

By now the narrative speed is timed to be as quick as the action of the poison will be. Ten lines is sufficient to kill off all three of the revellers, this suddenness having all the speed and finality of death about it, with the Pardoner stressing the extreme effects of the poison and citing medical authority in support. Having returned to his setpiece, he proceeds to the logical rhetorical flourish, the reiteration of the sins, the invocation embracing Christ and the wickedness of mankind. But, as I observed earlier, Chaucer is so *with* his creature that he makes us somewhat suspicious of the haste. Is it to try what he can get from this audience with whom he has been so tellingly honest? It is a gamble, but he unashamedly goes for the spoils – for aren't they there before him? It is a bold and brazen show, and although there are the moving lines already quoted ('And Iesu Crist, that is our soules leche') the Pardoner is not a one to hold back once the floodgates of his professional pride have been opened. In his own mind he has become the higher ecclesiastic he is aping and whose functions he is usurping, with his 'kneleth heer adoun, /And mekely receyveth my pardoun'. It is just possible that he has a moment of genuine feeling as indicated by the first quotation above, but he resumes his pose almost in reaction against it. We notice that after his preaching he becomes grotesquely, even hopefully, practical, seeing his role as useful to the pilgrims, of whom he is one. The irony is that these fellow pilgrims have probably placed the Pardoner well *beneath* them in their own minds. Such is the Pardoner's pride that he hits back by placing himself spiritually *above* them. One wonders if his invitation to the Host is born of snobbery. Be that as it may, the Host's words are coarse and real, the Knight's action in character, the author's single-line economy of continuation in keeping with the whole tale – compactly, tightly organized, displaying a variety of language, a sure narrative skill, embodying the artistic creed of the nineteenth-century novelist Henry James, total relevance. This section on Chaucer's art shows how closely Chaucer was able to identify with the character he created despite being out of sympathy with him. That mixture of colloquial language which has a ready appeal for his audience, with the learned references, images from nature, rhetorical flourishes which would be appreciated by a sermon-listening audience, who would perhaps also appreciate the structure of the Pardoner's 'sermon' too – all these mark Chaucer's achievement in *The Pardoner's Tale*. The final irony is that the success bears out the Pardoner's own words – 'For certes, many a predicacioun/Comth ofte tyme of yvel entencioun'.

Glossary

a–blakeberied: picking blackberries
a–two: in two
a–wey: away
aboght: paid for
abyde: live, endure
abyde: remain (line 435)
abye: pay for
accident: attribute (see textual note)
acorded: in agreement
actes: deeds
adversarie: foe
advocats: lawyers
affyle: make smooth
agayn: against
agayn: back (line 389)
agon: gone
agoon: ago
al: even though, if
al ones: at one, agreed
al–so: as (line 478)
alderbest: best of all
ale–stake: inn sign
algate: anyway
alle: all
allye: ally
alwey: always
amende: improve, reform
amis: wrongly

amy: companion
annexed: linked
anon: at once
apes: dupes, fools
artow: are you
arys: get up, rise up (in respect)
as: like
aspye: spy
assent: conspiracy
assoille: absolve
auctoritee: authority
avaryce: greed
avaunced: promoted
aventures: adventures
avicen: Avicenna (see textual note)
avow: swear
avysed: prepared
avyseth: consider
axe: ask
ay: always

bad: asked
bar: carried
bare: bareheaded
baudes: pimps
be: been (line 407)
begge: beg
bekke: nod (the head)
bel: good

bely: belly
ben (holde): known (as)
bench: seat
berd: beard
beried: buried
berne: barn
bestes: animals
bet: at once, quickly
beth: be
betwix: between
beye: purchase
bicched: cursed
bicomen: become
bifore: previously
biforn: in front of
bisinesse: work (at my work)
bityde: come to pass
biwreye: betray
bledinge: bleeding
blissed: blessed
blowe: ignite, fan (the flames)
blythe: gay, happy
body: person
boght(e): paid, redeemed
boist: box
bold: foolhardy
bones: dice (line 328)
boost: boast
borwed: borrowed
botels: bottles
bourde: joke
breech: breeches
breed: bread
bret-ful: brimful
bringe: accomplish
broches: brooches
broughte: held (line 474)
bulles: papal bulls, edicts

Burdeux: Bordeaux (France)
burdoun: refrain
busshels: bushels
but (for): except

caityf: wretch
can: know
canon: rule (see textual note)
capitayn: commander
capouns: chickens
cardiacle: heart attack
carl: churl
caryinge: removing
cast: planned
caste: throw
catel: goods
caught: had (words of the Host, line 27)
certes: certainly
chambre: room
chaunce: number for gambling on (line 325)
chaunge: exchange
Chepe: Cheapside
chere: mood, heart
cherl: villain
chese: cheese
cheste: chest of clothes
cink: five
circumstances: means
citee: town
cleer: innocent
clene: pure (line 586)
clepeth: call
clerk: scholar
clinke: chime
clout: shroud (line 408)
cloutes: rags

cod: bag
coillons: testicles
cokes: cooks
cokewold: cuckold
colpons: portions
comaunded: commanded
come: fall upon
commune: common
compeer: close friend,
  companion
comth: springs from
confiture: preparation,
  mixture
confusion: ruin
conseil: secret
contrarie: reverse of
contree: country
Corinthe: Corinth (one of the
  Greek city states)
corn: grain
corny: strong
corpus: body (used in oaths)
cors: body, corpse
cost: expense
counterfete: imitate
coveityse: greed
craft: trade
creatour: creator (God)
crepeth: finds, creeps
cristal: glass
Cristes: Christ's
croked: crooked
croys: cross
cure: care, concern
curs: curse
cursednesse: sin, vice(s)
curteisye: politeness
cut: lots

dame: mother
dampnable: meriting damnation
dampnacioun: damnation
dar: dare
debate: preach
deceyve: deceive
dede: deed
deed: dead
dees: dice
defame: dishonour
defaute: lapse
defended: forbidden
defenden: forbid
delyces: delicacies
delyt: delight
departed: shared
depeint: stained
dere: dearly
desolaat: disgraced
destourbe: hinder
destroyed: injured
develes: devil's
devocioun: devotion, devoutness,
  religious fervour
devyse: conceive (words of the
  Host, line 4)
devyse: outline
deyde: dead
deyntee: delicate
diden: were doing
digne: noble
dignitee: nobility
dischevele: with hair hanging
  loose
disfigured: distorted
dishonour: indignity
displesances: offences, injuries
doghtres: daughters

dome: judgement
dominacioun: control
donge: muck
doon: achieved (line 249)
doon: committed
doon us honge: have us hanged
dooth: does
doth: does
doutelees: undoubtedly
dowve: dove
draughte: measure
drawe: come, drawn
drede: doubt
dronkelewe: drunk
dryve: while (away)
dye: die

ecclesiaste: churchman, religious officer
ech: each
echoon: each one
eek: also
eet: ate
eldres: ancestors
elles: else
empoisoning: poisoning
ending: death
Engelond: England
ensamples: illustrative tales
entente: intention
entre: enter
envoluped: covered
er: before
erme (*my herte*): move me
erst er: before
estaat: status
ete: eaten
everich: each one

everichon: every one
evermore: always, from now on
expresly: exactly

fader: father
fair(e): fine
falle: fallen
fallest: fall down
fals(e): treacherous
falsnesse: lying
faste: near
fasting: fast, abstain from food
fayn: glad
feend: devil (Satan)
feith: faith
felawe: friend, mate
felaweship: companionship
felicitee: happiness
fen: section (see textual note)
fest: fist
feste: feast
fetys: graceful
fey: faith
feyned: imitation
fil: fell
finde: provide
first: prime
flaterye: flattery, lies
flex: flax
florins: valuable coins
folwen: result
folye: sin
fond: found
for: by (line 176)
for: of (line 123)
for-dronke: dead drunk
for-why: because

forby: past
forlete: lose, die
fors: matter
forswering: false oaths
forsweringes: perjury
forther: further
forwrapped: wrapped up
foul: loathsome
freendes: friend's
frendes: friends
fruyt: result
fruytesteres: fruitsellers
ful: completely
fulfild: overfull
fulfille: satisfy
fumositee: fumes, vapour
fundement: excrement

Galianes: probably drinks named after Galen (see textual note)
game: jest
gan: began
gat: obtained
gaude: trick
gelding: neutered or castrated horse
gentil: superior
gentils: nobles, refined ones
gete: provide (line 192)
giltelees: innocent
giternes: stringed instruments
glaringe: glaring
glas: glass
glotoun: glutton
gobet: small portion
god yow see: God be with you
gode: sound

golet: gullet
gon: gone
gonne: began
good: valuable (line 164)
goon: go
goon a pass: walk at a steady pace
goot: goat
governaunce: government
grace: favour, luck
graunte: agree, pledge
greet: great
grette: greeted
grettest: great men
greyn: grain
grisly: hideous, offensive
grotes: coins worth very little

habitacioun: dwelling
han: have
happed(e): happened
harrow: a cry of distress
hasard: gambling
hasardour: gambler
hasardrye: gambling
hath: draws (line 467)
haunteden: practised
haunteth: lives for
hauteyn: loud and elevated
hawe: yard
Hayles: Hales (see textual note)
heed: head
heigh: great
heighe: almighty
heleth: cures
hem: them, those
heng: hung
henne: from here

hente: called, catch, take
her: their
herd: heard
here: listen to
herkneth: listen
Herodes: Herod (see textual note)
herte: mind (words of the Host, line 4)
heste: command
hestes: commandments
hewe: appearance
heyre: haircloth
hir: her, their, with them
hogges: pig's
holde: retain, remember
holden: held to be
holy: pious
holynesse: virtue
homicide: murder
hond: hand
honest: decent
hool: recovered
hoom: home
hoor: white, grey
hoot: hot, fresh
hord: hoard
housbond: husband
hyer: greater
hyne: labourer

Iapes: tricks, stories (falsehoods)
Iet: fashion, style
Iewes: (the) Jews
Inde: India
Iolitee: greater comfort, display
Ioly: pretty

Iordanes: chamber pots
Ioye: pleasure
Ire: anger
Iustyse: magistrate
Iustyse: the dispensing of justice (line 259)

kepe: note, heed
kepe (fro): avoid
kepen: guard
knave: servant
kneleth: kneel
knokke: knock

Lacidomie: Sparta (Greek city state)
lafte: left
Lamuel: Lemuel (see textual note)
lasse: shorter
lasse (the): decline
laste: finally
lat cutte: let (them) be cut
late: recently
latoun: latten, brass, pinchbeck, base metal
leche: healer
leef: desirous
leef: leaves
leet: let
lenger: longer
Lepe: Spanish town (see textual note)
lere: learn
lese: lose
lesinges: lies, deception
lessoun: lesson

let: if
letuarie: medicines
leve: dear (line 403)
leve: permission, the right
lever: rather
leveth: abandon
lewed: common
licour: juice
lige (*lordes*): bishop
lightly: easily
likerous: greedy
livestow: have you lived
loketh: look, consult
lokkes: locks of hair
lond: country, in the
londes: lands
longe: large
look: make sure (line 502)
lordings: (ladies and) gentlemen
lost: overcome
Loth: Lot (see textual note)
lough: laughed, were laughing
lustes: desires
luxurie: lechery, lustfulness
lyf: life
lyking: liking, taste, wish
lyvinge: way of life

maister: master
make: give (line 218)
maken: make
maketh: ensure (line 190)
maladyes: illnesses
male: bag
maner (*pley*): diversions, ways of passing the time
manslaughtre: killing
mark: coins worth a great deal

mary: marrow
matere: subject
Mathew: St Matthew
mekely: humbly
meriely: cheerfully
mery: merry, happy
mesurable: moderate
might: may be (possible), ought to
mighte (*be*): was possible
mirthe: happy, happiness
mistriste: doubt
miteyn: mitten, glove
mo: more
moder: mother
modres: mother's
more and lasse: great and less (i.e. nobles and those of low birth)
moste: must
mot: might
mountance: amount
mowe: may
moyste: fresh
myle: mile
myn: my

na-more: no more
name: good name, reputation (line 283)
namely: especially, particularly
nat: not
natheles: nevertheless
nayles: nails (on the cross)
nedeth: is necessary, need
never-a-del: not at all
newe: latest
newe and newe: again and again

newer: renewed
niste: did not know
no-thing: in no way
noble: fine
nobles: gold coins
noght: not
non: no, none
noon: none
noon: no (line 417)
ny: nearly

o: one (line 245)
offertorie: the part of the service when the offering was made
officeres: servants
offre: offers
offren: offer
ofte: often
oghte: ought
ook: oak
oon: one, the same
oon assent: mutual agreement
or elles: alternatively
ordre: order, sequence (line 317)
original: origin
otes: oats
othes: oaths
otheres: others
ounces: in little bits
out (of): free from
out of: without (line 494)
out-cast: cast out
outrely: completely
over: more
overspradde: spread out
owene: own
oweth: owns

page: serving-boy
par cas: by chance
pardee: in truth
pardoun: pardons
parten (nat): be visited on
partest: leave
Parthes: Parthia
passe (over): forget
patente: licence
Paulus: St Paul
pees (holde): keep quiet
pens: pennies
peraventure: mischance
peril: dangerous
persevereth: remains, continues
person: parson
pestilence: plague
peyne: misery
peyne: take trouble, take pains
pilwe-beer: pillow case
pitee: compassion
pitous: pitying
pitously: compassionately
plat: plainly
plentee: great amount
plesaunce: providing pleasure
pleye: have fun, joke
pleye (falsly): cheat
pleyinge: occupied
pleyne: complain
plight: pledged
pokkes: pox
polcat: polecat
policye: administration
potage: soup
pothecarie: chemist
povert: poverty
povre: poor

povrest: poorest
power: authority
predicacioun: preaching, sermon
prelat: bishop
preyed: asked
principal: main
privee: latrine, urinal
privee: secret (line 347)
prively: secretly
profit: advantage
propre: fine
proudest: most arrogant
prow: good
pryde: pride
pryme: one of the seven canonical hours, about six in the morning
putte: place

quelle: destroy
quod: said
quyte: repay

rage: fit
rattes: rats
receyve: receive
rede: advise (line 465)
rede: have read
rede: red
redily: quickly
redy: ready
reed: advice
rekke: care
relikes: relics
renne: run
rente: wounded
repaireth: returned
replet: full of

reporte: repeat, talk about
reprevable: to be comdemned
repreve: shame, disgrace
reputacioun: estimation
resoun: reasonable, fairly
restelees: finding no rest
ribaudye: filthiness, scurrility
riden: rode
right: just
rightwisnesse: righteousness
Rochel: La Rochelle (France)
rolle: list
rolleth (*up and doun*): turned over
Ronyan: possibly an error for St Ninian (see textual note)
rote: heart
rote: roots
round: clearly
ryot: debauchery
ryotoures: revellers, riotous men
ryseth: rises
ryve: pierce

saffron: season
Sampsoun: Samson (see textual note)
saugh: saw
save: apart from (line 390)
save: protect (line 532)
scabbe: skin disease (in sheep)
see: sea
seel: seal
seint Eleyne: St Helena (see textual note)
seintuarie: sacred box
seith: tells
sely: innocent

seme: appear

semeth: seems to come

Senek: Seneca

sepulture: tomb

sermone: preach

set: sitting down

seuretee: reassurance

seyde: said

seye: say

seye (*this worde*): talk of this subject

seyl: sail

seyn: observe, say (line 461)

shape: contrive

shewe: display

sholde: should

sholder-boon: shoulder bone

shoop him: planned

shorte: small

shortly (*for to sayn*): to put it briefly

shrewe: wretch

shryned: enshrined

shul: shall

shuldres: shoulders

signes: hints

sith: since, then

sleen: kill, slay

sleeth: kills

smal: feeble

smale: small

smerte: sharp

smoot: burst

so: provided, such

sobrenesse: a sober manner

soghte: looked through, read

somme: every one

sondry: various

song: sung

sooth: truth

sore: deeply

soun: sound

sour: foul

sovereyn: greatest, main

sowed: sewn

sowen: sown

spak: spoke

spake: spoke

special: particular

spere: spear

spicerye: spices

spones: spoons

stal: stole

sterlinges: silver pennies

sterte: started

sterve: die, starve

stewes: brothels

stif: strong bass voice

stiked: stuck

stire: encourage

stonde: stand

stondeth: stands, is set down

stones: boxes or jars (line 19)

stones: jewels (line 31, General Prologue)

stoor: livestock

storven: dies

streight: just, directly

strenger: stronger

streyne: strain

strike: hank

strogelest: wrestle

stryving: quarrelling

substaunce: essential quality (see textual note)

subtilly: cunningly, subtly

suffisant: competent
suffyse: suffice
superfluitee: excesses (sensual)
swelle: becomes swollen, ill
swich(e): such
swinke: toil
swyn: pig
swythe: quickly
sydes: sides

table: tablet
take: refer to (line 155)
taken: had (as lovers)
talent: inclination
tarie: delay
taverner: publican
teche: teachings
tellen: relate
terme, (in): in technical terms
theech: may I prosper
theef: thief
theen: prosper
ther-biforn: previously
therby: in that way
theves: thieves
thider: thither
thilke: the same, this
thise: these
tho: these
thogh: if
thoughte: calculated (line 443)
thridde: third
thurgh: through
thyne: your
to-swinke: labour, toil
to-tere: tear (apart)
togidres: together
tombesteres: dancing girls

tonge: tongue
tood: travelled, rode
tord: turd
torn: turn
tresor: treasure
trespased: caused harm
trespasse: sins
trete: deal with, teach
tretee: treaty
trewe: genuine
trewely: really, certainly, truthfully
treye: three
triacle: medicine
troden: got
trompe: trumpet, trumpeter
trone: throne, seat of judgement
trouthe: honour
trowe: believe, think
trussed: folded
turnen: turn
tweye: two
twinne: turn

unbokel: undo
understondeth: understands
unkinde: unnatural
unkindely: unnaturally
unwitingly: unknowingly
up-on: in
urinals: vessels for holding urine
usage: habit
use: practise

vanish: fade
venim: poison

vernicle: a badge of St Veronica
  (see textual note)
verray: real
veyl: veil
veyne (*glorie*): empty pride
vicious: unprincipled
vileinye: rudeness, villainy
visage: face
voys: voice
vyce: sin
vyne: vine

walet: bag
walken: are about
war: wary
ware: warn
warente: protect
warne: warn
waryce: heal
wash: bathe
wasshe: dipped
wast: waste
wel: correctly (line 341)
welked: withered
wenche: girl
wende: go along
wende: would have thought
wenen: believe
weneth: believes, thinks
weping: weeping
wered: wore
wex: wax
wey: path
weyes: ways
whennes: whence, from where
whete: wheat
who-so: whosoever
whyl: while

whyle: time
whyle: as long as
whylom: once upon a time
widwe: widow
wight: person
wike: week
wil: desire
wilfully: deliberately
wiste: knew, knows
wit: intelligence (line 450)
wit: senses (line 231)
wit: wisdom
with sory grace: bad luck to
  you/him
witnesse: evidence
wo: suffering
wol: will
wolde: would wish
wolle: wool
wombe: stomach
wonder: wondrous
wonne: gained
wont: accustomed
wood: mad
woodnesse: madness
woost: know
woot: know
wot: knows
wrappe: wrap
wrecchednesse: misery
wreke (*him*): revenge
  himself
wroghte: made, was doing
wrooth: angry
wyf: wife
wyn: wine
wyn-yeving: wine-giving
wys: wise

wyse: manner
wysly: discreetly, cleverly

y-boren: born, true-born
y-caried: be moved
y-coyned: coined
y-crammed: filled
y-falle: have fallen in with
y-fallen: occurring
y-graunted: invested in
y-hent: seized
y-holde: held, judged
y-maad: made
y-maked: be made
y-set: seated
y-shave: shaved

y-shriven: confessed, received forgiveness
y-slawe: killed
y-slayn: was killed
y-stonge: stung
y-wis: certainly
yaf: gave
ydel: casual
ydelly: in vain
yeer: year
yerne: briskly
yeve: give
yeven: given
yiftes: gifts
yow: you
Ypocras: spicy-flavoured wine
yvel: evil

Discussion Topics

Your understanding and appreciation of *The Pardoner's Tale* will be much increased if you discuss aspects of it with other people. Here are some topics you could consider:

1. Imagine you are one of the pilgrims listening to the Pardoner. Do you think you would find him impressive and sincere or not?
2. What do the examples of human sinfulness used by the Pardoner contribute to the main themes of his tale?
3. Which do you prefer, the Pardoner's own address to the audience, or the story of the three rioters, and why?
4. Say what you find humorous in *The Pardoner's Tale*.
5. How far do you think the Host is justified in his attitude towards the Pardoner?
6. Discuss Chaucer's ability to use dialogue in the tale. What effects would this have on the listeners (in the audience) and the readers (you and me?)

The GCSE Examination

In this examination you may find that the set texts have been selected by your teacher from a very wide list of suggestions in the examination syllabus. The questions in the examination paper will therefore be applicable to many different books. Here are some questions which you could answer by making use of *The Pardoner's Tale*:

1. Select a book or story which has a very strong moral or theme, and explain clearly what it is and how the author presents it.
2. Write about a novel or play in which one of the leading characters is intent upon profit or self-interest to the exclusion of everything else.

3. Choose an incident or situation from a book you have been studying which is either (a) exciting, and which leads to death, or (b) has an atmosphere of tension.
4. Write about a book you have read which is dominated by one character and his or her attempts to influence others.
5. Choose a book which contains a story within the main story (perhaps told by one of the characters, or which refers to a past situation) and write it out in some detail. What did it contribute to your appreciation of the book?
6. Write about an incident in any book you have read in which one person is the focus of contempt *or* ridicule *or* hostility *or* fear.

Questions on *The Pardoner's Tale*

1. Write a clear account of the methods employed by the Pardoner in seeking to hold his audience's attention.
2. By close attention to detail in the text, show how the story of the three revellers illustrates the main theme of *The Pardoner's Tale*.
3. Write a character study of the Pardoner himself based on evidence from the Tale.
4. Write about one aspect of the Tale which you find particularly interesting (e.g., the old man, Chaucer's economy of language, etc.).
5. Write an essay on Chaucer's use of irony (i.e., the tone which makes it clear that the Pardoner is 'conning' his audience).
6. Write down what you learn of life in Chaucer's England from *The Pardoner's Tale*.

FOR THE BEST IN PAPERBACKS, LOOK FOR THE

In every corner of the world, on every subject under the sun, Penguin represents quality and variety – the very best in publishing today.

For complete information about books available from Penguin – including Pelicans, Puffins, Peregrines and Penguin Classics – and how to order them, write to us at the appropriate address below. Please note that for copyright reasons the selection of books varies from country to country.

In the United Kingdom: For a complete list of books available from Penguin in the U.K., please write to *Dept E.P., Penguin Books Ltd, Harmondsworth, Middlesex, UB7 0DA*

In the United States: For a complete list of books available from Penguin in the U.S., please write to *Dept BA, Penguin, 299 Murray Hill Parkway, East Rutherford, New Jersey 07073*

In Canada: For a complete list of books available from Penguin in Canada, please write to *Penguin Books Canada Ltd, 2801 John Street, Markham, Ontario L3R 1B4*

In Australia: For a complete list of books available from Penguin in Australia, please write to the *Marketing Department, Penguin Books Australia Ltd, P.O. Box 257, Ringwood, Victoria 3134*

In New Zealand: For a complete list of books available from Penguin in New Zealand, please write to the *Marketing Department, Penguin Books (NZ) Ltd, Private Bag, Takapuna, Auckland 9*

In India: For a complete list of books available from Penguin, please write to *Penguin Overseas Ltd, 706 Eros Apartments, 56 Nehru Place, New Delhi, 110019*

In Holland: For a complete list of books available from Penguin in Holland, please write to *Penguin Books Nederland B.V., Postbus 195, NL–1380AD Weesp, Netherlands*

In Germany: For a complete list of books available from Penguin, please write to *Penguin Books Ltd, Friedrichstrasse 10 – 12, D–6000 Frankfurt Main 1, Federal Republic of Germany*

In Spain: For a complete list of books available from Penguin in Spain, please write to *Longman Penguin España, Calle San Nicolas 15, E–28013 Madrid, Spain*